Managing
Financial
Information

David Davies is principal lecturer in financial management
at the University of Portsmouth. A qualified accountant
with a masters degree in management from Henley
Management College, he previously spent 17 years in the
private and public sectors with GEC, Thomas De la Rue,
IBM and several local authorities. He currently lectures on
DPM, MBA, DMS and undergraduate courses as well as
undertaking consultancy work.

Other titles in the series:

*Core Personnel and
Development*
Mick Marchington and
Adrian Wilkinson

Employee Development
2nd edition
Rosemary Harrison

Employee Relations
2nd edition
John Gennard and
Graham Judge

Employee Resourcing
Stephen Taylor

Employee Reward
2nd edition
Michael Armstrong

*Essentials of
Employment Law*
6th edition
David Lewis and
Malcolm Sargeant

Managing Activities
Michael Armstrong

*Managing in a Business
Context*
David Farnham

*Managing Information
and Statistics*
Roland and Frances Bee

Managing People
Jane Weightman

Personnel Practice
2nd edition
Malcolm Martin and
Tricia Jackson

The Chartered Institute of Personnel and Development is the
leading publisher of books and reports for personnel and
training professionals, students, and all those concerned with
the effective management and development of people at work.
For details of all our titles, please contact the Publishing
Department:

tel. 020-8263 3387
fax 020-8263 3850
e-mail publish@cipd.co.uk

The catalogue of all CIPD titles can be viewed on the CIPD
website:

www.cipd.co.uk/publications

PEOPLE AND ORGANISATIONS

Managing Financial Information

DAVID DAVIES

Chartered Institute of Personnel and Development

First published in 1999
Reprinted 2000, 2001

Design by Curve

Typeset by Fakenham Photosetting Ltd, Fakenham, Norfolk

Printed in Great Britain by
the Cromwell Press, Trowbridge, Wiltshire

British Library Cataloguing in Publication Data
A catalogue record of this book is available from the British Library

ISBN 0-85292-782-7

Chartered Institute of Personnel and Development, CIPD House,
Camp Road, London SW19 4UX
Tel: 020-8971 9000   Fax: 020-8263 3333
E-mail: cipd@cipd.co.uk Website: www.cipd.co.uk
Incorporated by Royal Charter. Registered Charity No. 1079797.

Contents

FOREWORD   VI

1 Introduction   1
2 The finance function and the personnel manager   9
3 The personnel manager and management information
  systems   20
4 The balance sheet and the personnel manager   28
5 The trading and profit and loss account and the
  personnel manager   38
6 The manufacturing account and the personnel
  department   54
7 The interpretation and use of financial information for
  personnel   61
8 Financial implications of personnel decisions   78
9 Costing and human resources   83
10 Absorption costing   88
11 Standard costing   97
12 Marginal costing and personnel decisions   106
13 The personnel manager and the planning system   113
14 The cash budget   122
15 The master budget   129
16 Capital budgeting and its application to personnel   136

APPENDIX
Discounted cash flow: selected tables   144
Solutions to problems and exercises   146

GLOSSARY   169

BIBLIOGRAPHY   174

PROFESSIONAL STANDARDS INDEX   175

INDEX   176

Foreword

Welcome to this series of texts designed to complement the Core Management syllabus. The role of the personnel and development practitioner has become an important part of the total management of all types of organisation in the private, public and voluntary sectors. A fundamental element of that role is the ability to comprehend and contribute to the overall goals, performance and outcomes of organisations. This is the purpose of the Core Management syllabus: to equip personnel and development practitioners to understand and appreciate complex business and managerial issues and to develop their skills so that they can play a full role in that process.

One of the major issues facing personnel and development professionals is the extent to which financial data have become part of the manager's life. Whether in the private or the public sector, managers are now faced with budgetary decisions at increasingly devolved levels of operation. It is essential, therefore, for individual practitioners to be able to comprehend financial data, work with financial information and appreciate the implications and consequences of decisions that have a major impact on the financial viability of their organisation. This text provides a framework and the materials for financial management in a range of organisational settings.

Professor Ian J Beardwell
Head, Department of HRM
Leicester Business School
De Montfort University
Leicester

1 Introduction

Organisations require many resources to enable them to operate successfully in an environment that is competitive and frequently openly hostile. In the private sector, organisational success can be measured in different ways, including the organisation's ability to make profits, generate cash, capture greater market share or provide a service more effectively than its competitors. The public sector has often found difficulty in justifying the work that it undertakes on the grounds that there is 'no profit motive'. This has dramatically changed in recent years, with value-for-money audits, the need for direct-works organisations to compete in the open market for contracts, and the application of compulsory competitive tendering to all parts of the organisation. Such was the enthusiasm with which all this was followed that there was some concern that the public sector would disappear entirely.

In looking at the financial information systems available to help organisations in decision-making, planning and control, however, it is impossible to ignore the fact that there is a legal framework within which they must operate, irrespective of whether they are in the public or the private sector. There are constraints relating to terms and conditions of employment, unfair dismissal and equal opportunities, all of which generally come under the auspices of the personnel manager, as do disciplinary and grievance procedures. The purpose of this Introduction is to show a little of the legal framework, but company law is an extremely important area: more detailed coverage is to be found in the books that make up the IPD's *Legal Essentials* series.

THE PRIVATE SECTOR

This comprises three types of business organisation: sole traders, partnerships, and companies.

Sole traders

This type of organisation, as the name implies, consists of a single individual who takes full responsibility for all the work that is undertaken. If things go well and the business is successful, all the profits can be used as the proprietor chooses. On the other hand, if things go badly and losses are incurred, all his or her personal effects, including the family home (if he or she owns it individually or in part), can be sold to repay creditors.

A sole trader can commence business at any time, with few formalities. It is, however, usual to register for value-added tax (VAT) and to obtain any necessary planning permission for the premises used. If the owner wishes to feature a company name that differs from his or her own name, the Business Names Act 1985 has to be complied with. The business ceases with the death or retirement of the owner.

Partnerships

A partnership consists of two or more people who agree to carry on a business, sharing profits and losses in proportions that are part of the same agreement. The partnership agreement may be purely verbal but is usually in writing. It sets out not only the way in which profits and losses are to be shared, but also the salaries to be received by the partners. A partnership, like a sole trader, can start business at any time with few formalities other than the necessity of obtaining any necessary planning permission for premises, registering for VAT, and complying with the Business Names Act 1985.

The death of a partner can lead to the dissolution of the partnership, but the agreement more usually provides for the business to continue under the remaining partner(s). It will be necessary for the continuing partner(s) to buy out the share of the deceased, and there may then be problems in raising the required finance. The basic rules that apply to a partnership are embodied in the Partnership Act 1890, which, together with the general law of the land, governs its activities.

Companies

There are two types of company: the limited company (Ltd), which does not offer its shares to the general public, and the public limited company (plc), shares in which are offered to the public at large through the medium of the Stock Exchange. Both types consist of two or more people incorporated as a registered company, who become its shareholders and who appoint directors to manage the company and act as its agents. The shareholders must also officially appoint a company secretary. The company cannot commence business until the formalities have been completed. These include a certificate of incorporation from the Registrar of Companies, compliance with the Companies Act 1985 and with the Business Names Act 1985 and, usually, registration for VAT.

A company is a legal entity separate from its owners, and its existence is unaffected by the death or retirement of any of them. On the other hand, it has a far more complex legal framework within which to operate than either the sole trader or the partnership. It has an obligation to file accounts annually, together with the directors' and auditors' reports. These items are retained by the Registrar of Companies and are available for inspection on request from Companies House. Annual general meetings (AGMs) must be held so that shareholders are kept informed of corporate activities which must accord with the articles and memorandum of association that set out the limits of the company's activities in pursuance of its trade.

THE PUBLIC SECTOR

This comprises three types of organisation: commercial public organisations, social service organisations, and local government organisations.

Commercial public organisations

These receive their authority (and their constraints) from the national government and are run on commercial lines under the control of a government minister.

[Handwritten margin notes:]

you have to be a member of stock exchange to do this. Those who are not may sell shares through banks.

limited companys tend to be formed so they can be protected by limited liability.

until you have this — considered a partnership — then you are all jointly liable if you go into liquidation.

A plc must have issued £50,000 Shares

Social service organisations

These also receive their authority from the national government, on whose behalf they run a social service, such as the Health and Safety Executive.

The commercial public corporations and social service organisations are each a separate legal entity, and their objects and powers are defined by the Act of Parliament that created them.

Local authorities

These derive their powers (and limitations) from the Acts of Parliament and charters that created them. They have a great many obligatory duties and enormous delegatory powers, but they must take great care that they do nothing that is *ultra vires* – ie outside their authority – for if they do they have to pay for the consequences. They are independent within the powers authorised by national government.

The public-sector organisations employ large numbers of people, so that the death or retirement of an individual has no effect on their existence. They have a statutory duty to account for the manner in which they discharge their responsibilities and must appoint auditors to report on the activities of the period under review. Accounts have to be prepared for the national government that are open to inspection by the general public. In recent years the Westminster government's concern to obtain value for money has put local authorities under close public scrutiny. As a result, they are considered to have become more efficient.

The conditions under which such concerns operate are complex, and all the concerns are restricted in what they are legally entitled to do. This makes it essential for them to take legal advice at the time they are established, in order to ensure that the purpose for which they have been set up is a legitimate one. The personnel manager has an important role in monitoring that the conditions of employment are fully met so helping to enable such organisations to enjoy the confidence of the general public that they serve.

The current fiscal climate tends to mean that the public and private sectors have to compete for scarce resources to enable them to operate at all, and if organisations and corporations are to grow they have to be seen to be performing successfully in order to attract those resources. Both sectors require people, materials, equipment, buildings, money and information. Although each of these is important, this book is mostly concerned with how the personnel manager obtains and uses financial resources for the benefit of the organisation. The decisions of such managers and others are translated into the international language of money, which provides a basis for a common understanding of plans and enables the performance of organisations, and of individuals within those organisations, to be monitored and controlled. This cannot be achieved, however, without frequent and accurate financial information in the right form that reaches the right people at the right time to enable them to make good use of it. Personnel managers, among many others, need to keep a close eye on the cash position. The way in which money moves through a manufacturing concern may be illustrated by the way in which water flows through a circuit of reservoirs and pipes (Figure 1).

The reservoirs of inventory (ie raw materials, stock), capital, work in progress, finished goods and debtors represent 'banks' in which money may build up. If they are allowed to become too large, cash-flow problems will result. The management information system should therefore highlight these prospective problems, so that management is made aware of them early enough for remedial action to be taken to correct the situation before it becomes serious. Good management practice – which is represented by the pumps (ie the circles in Figure 1) – supported by useful, timely information, ensures that any delays which occur are kept to an absolute minimum. The personnel manager can contribute to cash-flow management by helping to ensure that an efficient credit controller is appointed, thus helping to keep debt at a reasonable level.

The public sector is under exactly the same pressures to ensure that the best possible use is made of the people,

Figure 1 Where the money goes in a manufacturing concern

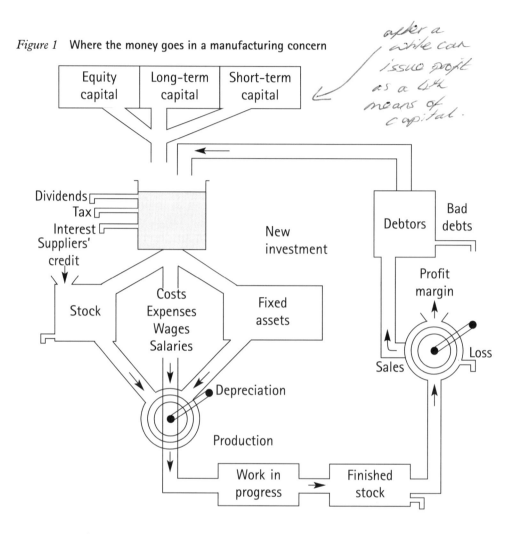

after a while can issue profit as a 4th means of capital.

money and other resources available to it, and that no hold-ups occur in the efficient running of the organisation.

Both sectors are responsible for planning their activities and controlling events as they take place so that targets are met and the instructions of management are carried out. Personnel managers ensure that the organisation's goals are achieved through its people. Failure to perform to the required standard leads to job losses and, possibly, the collapse of the organisation. Sources of finance may show a different emphasis: much of the public-sector money coming from the business rate, the Council Tax and government

Figure 2 Where the money goes in a non-manufacturing organisation

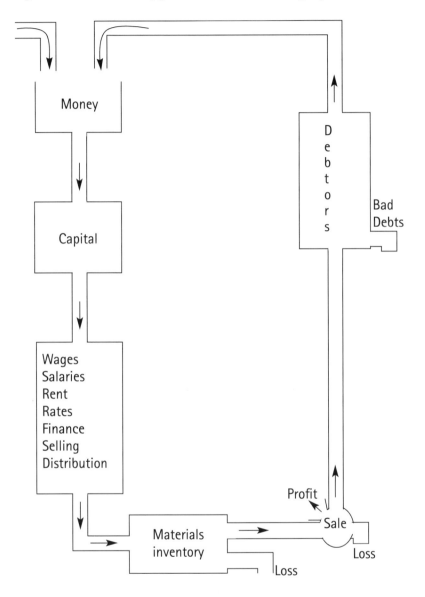

grants, whereas the private sector is responsible for obtaining its resources direct from the public. They both provide goods and services with the monies obtained, and compete in the provision of such services as old people's and children's homes, refuse collection and housing maintenance, as well as housing itself.

In view of this commonality, Figure 2 is appropriate to both the non-manufacturing private sector and the non-manufacturing public sector of the economy. We can see that for all organisations the control of levels of stock/inventory and debtors is extremely important. The ways in which this control may be achieved are discussed later in the book, but the efficiency of the organisation depends on the correct information's being available in the right place at the right time, and then being promptly acted upon by correctly trained people.

This book has been written to give personnel practitioners a clear understanding of the processes outlined above, and of the role of financial and cost accounts and how they may be employed to clarify the financial performance of organisations and aid decision-making.

The next two chapters explore the role of financial management. Chapters 4 to 8 discuss specific financial statements, and their use to the personnel manager, and the remainder of the book looks at the role of costing in the process of planning and control in which the personnel manager is involved.

2 The finance function and the personnel manager

By the end of this chapter the reader should understand the role of the finance function and its links with the personnel department. The management competencies that this chapter is intended to develop are those of monitoring and controlling the use of resources and of securing effective resource allocation for activities and projects.

ORGANISATIONAL FINANCE

It is important for a personnel manager to understand the role of the finance function in his or her organisation because a proportion of the finances obtained will of course be required by the personnel department. The financial manager is responsible for obtaining financial resources as cheaply as possible and ensuring that they are effectively employed by the organisation. Such employment is more likely to be achieved in the personnel department if the personnel manager and the financial manager work closely together towards a common goal. There are three main decisions that have to be made by the financial manager: on financing, on investment, and on asset management.

The financing decision

This is the first major decision of the organisation. What sources are to be used to obtain finance, and in what proportions? In the private sector the amount that can be raised by the issue of shares or by borrowing is limited by the Articles and Memorandum of Association. Nonetheless, the proportions in which the money is raised through the issues of shares or in other ways has an impact on the cost of the resources as well as on the public's perception of the firm. Companies that borrow a high proportion of their financial resources as opposed to issuing shares are said to be highly geared or leveraged, and are perceived to be high-risk

venture capitalist to put money into make profits (they will want part of the company)

Company financiers - different costs - Shareholders, Banks and long-term loans.

concerns. The most popular source of finance for existing companies in the private sector is internally-generated funds or retained profits.

The ways in which organisations in the public sector can obtain finance are laid down by statute and are constrained by the principle of *ultra vires*. This means that certain actions are beyond their powers, and sets boundaries within which the organisation must function. Nevertheless, the head of the financial department has a good deal of discretion in deciding where borrowed monies should be obtained, although there is obviously clear public accountability. The monies raised are used firstly to enable the organisation to continue to operate, and are allocated to department heads, including personnel managers, on the basis agreed in the budget. Secondly, they can be allocated to capital projects as discussed later in this book.

The investment decision

The second major decision is on how the funds that the organisation has obtained should be invested. Here again the private sector has rather more discretion than the public, which has a statutory duty to provide such services as public health and housing. The financial manager, in conjunction with the personnel manager and other members of the management team, has to decide how much should be invested in fixed assets like land and building, plant and machinery and equipment, and how much in current assets like inventory (ie raw materials) or stock.

long term benefit (invest as much as possible)

current period or next period only.

[working capital]

The asset management decision

The financial manager helps to decide how the assets that have been acquired should be managed. It is in the nature of organisations that once fixed assets have been obtained they remain *in situ* for several years. This tends to make managers concentrate their attention in the short term on current asset management (ie stock, debtors and cash).

overheads ↓ wages ↓ stock. (invest as little as possible)

The management team works in the management of the assets together with the personnel manager responsible for

equity share capital – pay shareholders dividends

managing both the normal departmental assets and the most valuable assets that any organisation possesses – its people. We cannot put an inventory value on people, but companies such as Marks & Spencer which makes special efforts to manage and motivate its staff invariably see the results coming through on the bottom line in the form of increased profits, although there are occasional hiccups as change takes place, as has been recently demonstrated.

The management information system

The financial manager has another important role to play: he or she operates the financial information system. Most organisations now have a computerised system that shows managers how well they are working to plan. This information is usually produced monthly, although it can be done more frequently, and it is the financial manager's responsibility to ensure that the information is up to date, received on time and accurate. It is no good informing the personnel manager that the department is £20,000 over budget three months after the end of the year to which the information relates. By then it is too late to take any remedial action.

The personnel, financial and other managers should discuss the information they require in order to run their departments effectively. (Examples of how finance fits into the overall organisational structure in the private sector and in a local authority are shown in Figure 3.) Once what is required is known, the timing and detail of the information should be agreed. It is no use for the system to produce a 30-page report if only four pages are being used – not only because it is a waste of paper but more importantly because it is an ineffective use of a manager's time to be looking at information that is not relevant to the job in hand.

Figure 3 shows that the financial manager is responsible for raising money as cheaply as possible and using it effectively within the context of the organisation that is being served. In order to achieve this the objective or goal of the organisation must be known so that the context within

Figure 3 Finance on the organisation chart

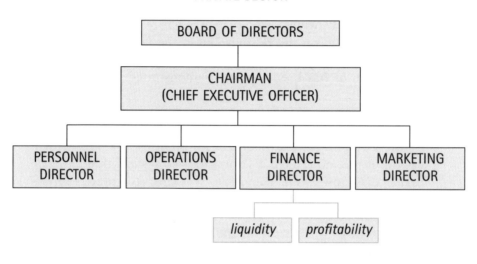

PRIVATE SECTOR

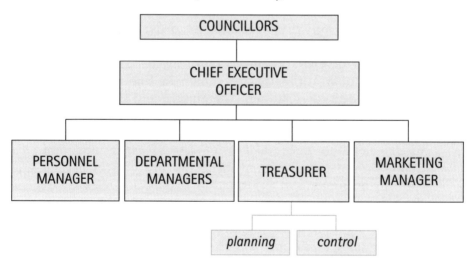

PUBLIC SECTOR
(local authority)

which the management is operating is clear. We will now accordingly look more closely at the sources from which money is obtained and the ways in which it can be employed.

 ## THE SOURCES AND USES OF CAPITAL

Figure 1 in Chapter 1 demonstrated the three types of finance required by organisations:

- permanent/equity capital
- long-term capital
- short-term capital

Permanent/equity capital

This is the money provided for the organisation by its owners which does not have to be repaid as long as the organisation continues as a going concern.

In the private sector the money provided by the owners is in the form of share capital, and profits that have been retained in the organisation, when it has traded successfully, become reserves. The share capital can be broken down into various type of shares. The ordinary share capital is the equity capital and gives the holder the right to vote on the way in which the organisation should operate. The wishes of the shareholders are carried out by their elected representatives, the board of directors, and each director is normally expected to hold a large number of ordinary shares in the company. Directors who did not hold a large number of shares could be viewed with suspicion, because it might seem that they had no confidence in the organisation they were running. The company is under no obligation to buy back any of the shares that it has sold, although it may decide to do so. The normal means of recovering money invested in an organisation through the purchase of shares is by selling those shares to a purchaser through the medium of the Stock Exchange.

The ordinary shareholders, or equity holders, carry the biggest risk of all those who provide money for an organisation. There is no stated rate of return on their investment, and if the company does not do well, they get no return. They are the last to receive a return on their investment and the last to be paid in the event of failure, ranking after all the other creditors, secured or unsecured.

Other shareholders who provide permanent capital are the preference shareholders who, as the name implies, are in a preferential position *vis-à-vis* the ordinary shareholders with regard to the receipt of dividends and the return of their money should the business fail. In view of this reduced risk, the preference shareholders do not normally have voting rights when major decisions concerning the running of the company are made. Preference shares, like ordinary shares, can be bought and sold through the Stock Exchange.

The purpose of the Stock Exchange is to act as a marketplace and bring together the providers and users of capital. Companies that wish to be listed on the Exchange must have a proven record of profitability over a number of years and submit to a thorough investigation by the Stock Exchange before the privilege is granted. Those companies that are listed find their ability to raise permanent capital greatly enhanced, provided market conditions are conducive to the issue of shares.

Companies that wish to raise money through the issue of shares usually make use of the services of an issuing house, which will give advice on the timing and size of the issue and the price at which the shares should be issued. Press advertisements give details of the issue and invite applications for the purchase of shares. Payment is normally required in more than one instalment or tranche. For example, if the shares were to be sold for £1.50 each, payment might be requested as 50p on application, 50p on first call and 50p on second and final call, so that it could be three or four years after they had been received that the shares are fully paid for. Individuals wishing to sell shares they already own may also use the Stock Exchange, but they then employ the services of a stockbroker rather than an issuing house.

The permanent capital having been raised, it is the responsibility of the management of the organisation to ensure that it is put to good use immediately. The purpose for which it was raised would have been stated at the time the public was invited to invest, and business should be started as quickly as possible if criticism that might make it difficult to raise money in the future is to be avoided.

Permanent capital is needed to build or expand an organisation through the purchase of fixed assets, such as plant and machinery, land and buildings, fixtures and fittings, or through the purchase of another company. On the other hand, it might be used to increase the working capital, which is what enables an undertaking to keep running until it earns some more money from its operations, and out of which all its running expenses are met.

Working capital is tied up in inventory (ie raw materials), debtors and the bank, and lack of it severely restricts an organisation's ability to operate successfully. An injection of fresh working capital can lead to increased operating levels, giving greater profitability and hence additional retained profits.

Long-term capital
The long-term capital consists of borrowed monies which will remain in the company for five or more years, and sometimes carries the option of being converted into ordinary share capital at the discretion of the lender. Normally, long-term loans are secured by a charge on the fixed assets of the borrowing concern, so that if things do not go well, the lenders are certain of recovering their money through the sale of the fixed assets if necessary. Only the most successful organisations, like Tesco or GEC, are able to raise loans that are not secured on their fixed assets, because lenders feel that their money is safe with them and that the conditions on which it was lent will be honoured in full.

Loans may be raised through the stock market, particularly if they are to be convertible loans, but more usually the services of the other institutions of the City of London are employed. It may be possible to raise money through one of the clearing banks, such as Barclays, Lloyds, Midland or NatWest, but it should be remembered that they are not normally providers of venture capital and look for absolute security in their lending. However, recent events, such as the Hedging Fund crisis in the USA and the overlending exposed by the 1987 recession, have demonstrated that they are not infallible.

More likely sources of long-term capital are the merchant banks, which specialise rather more in the provision of venture capital but would still demand an extremely close look at an organisation's prospects and available security before lending it any money. 3i (Investors in Industry) are the biggest suppliers of venture capital in the United Kingdom.

The pension funds are always looking for good investment opportunities, but they too prefer safe investments, both from the point of view of income – that is, the dividend received – and from that of capital growth – the increase in the value of the investment. They are prohibited from the simple lending of money. The Business Expansion Scheme also exists to bring together organisations that require capital and those prepared to provide it, facilitated by special tax provisions to attract the providers of capital. This now seems to be nearing the end of its useful life due to changes in the tax laws.

These are the main providers of long-term capital, but there are others. It should be remembered that wherever the capital is obtained, the lender will need to be assured of its safety. The less security there is, the higher the charge for the money is – if it can be obtained at all. A secured loan may be obtained at 5 per cent, but an unsecured loan could cost as much as 13 per cent, and to make that worth while, the user should ensure that at least 16 per cent is being earned – that is, a 3 per cent profit on top of the loan amount – a requirement beyond most organisations.

Borrowed money can be used either externally or internally – ie to repay previous borrowings outside the company or, within the organisation, to enable it to operate more effectively. Whatever is done must be perceived to be to the benefit of the borrowing organisation; otherwise, it will prove to be both difficult and expensive to raise further funds in the future.

Short-term capital

Short-term capital, in the form of loans that have to be repaid within five years, can be raised from the same sources and on broadly similar terms as long-term capital, although there are differences in the rate of interest charged. The expertise of the financial management function is tested when borrowing money in that it is its job to obtain the best possible terms even while the lenders are endeavouring to get the best possible terms for themselves. When interest rates are high, lenders will want to lend for as long as possible and at a fixed rate of interest, whereas the borrower will want the loan to be for as short a term as possible and at a variable rate of interest, in the expectation that it will quickly fall.

The amount of borrowing and the terms on which money is lent will be decided largely by the City's view of the organisation and its present capital structure – that is to say, the proportion of borrowed money in relation to the capital put up by the owners. If the proportion of borrowing is large, the organisation is said to be 'highly geared', and it may be extremely difficult for it to borrow any further money.

The question of 'gearing' is complex, but it can be said that the more highly geared an organisation is, the greater the risk a prospective lender is taking and the higher the return that will be expected. A general rule in relation to the use of borrowed monies is that 'you do not borrow short to invest long'. This means that short-term borrowing should not be invested in fixed assets, because if it were, it might be necessary to sell the fixed assets when the time came to repay the loan. Generally short-term borrowing should be employed in short-term investment, so that the money can if necessary be obtained easily when it has to be repaid.

The principles apply to both the private and the public sectors when they wish to raise money through the marketplace, except that local authorities are generally regarded as more secure places in which to invest money. Nonetheless they still have to compete in terms of interest.

The proportion of funds that is obtained directly through the institutions of the City of London varies between the public and private sectors, in that a large proportion of the money obtained by local government comes through the Council Tax, the business rate, and government grants. Figure 4 shows how Portsmouth City Council was funded in 1998–99.

Figure 4 Portsmouth City Council funding

	%
Contribution from balances and reserves	5
Revenue Support grant	48
Business rate	27
Collection fund	20

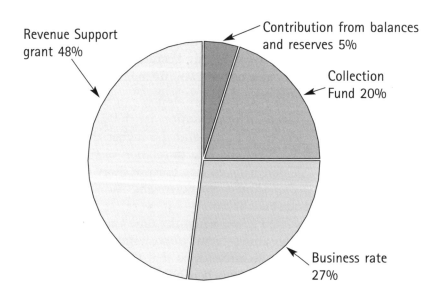

What is share capital?

What is a dividend? *The return that is expected by a shareholder which is the income on the share.*

What is inventory or stock? *raw materials stock, WIP stock, finished goods stock.*

What are the three major decisions that have to be made by the financial manager? *Finance, Investment & Asset management decisions.*

What is a fixed asset?

Ascertain how your organisation obtains its financial resources and the basis on which they are allocated to the personnel department.

3 The personnel manager and management information systems

At the end of this chapter the reader should understand financial information systems and how they can be used by the personnel manager. The competencies this chapter is intended to develop are those of evaluating proposals for expenditure and controlling expenditure in relation to budgets.

The environment in which organisations operate is so complex that it would be impossible for them to survive without detailed planning, monitoring and information from a great variety of sources. It follows, therefore, that organisations must set up information systems that are helpful to the managers in running the operations for which they are responsible. This chapter looks at some of the financial information systems that are available to the personnel manager: they are discussed in greater detail later in this book.

In planning it is necessary to have information: no plan can be devised in a vacuum. The bulk of this information is in most organisations derived from actions that have taken place in the past. Management looks at what has been happening over the last five years, with particular emphasis on the last year. Then, with the aid of economic forecasts and reports from its own sources, it attempts to forecast what will happen to the organisation over the next five or six years. It is extremely unlikely that any of these forecasts will be 100-percent accurate even for the next year – but there is no doubt that the more information there is available, the more accurate the forecast is likely to be.

Organisations that are new and making their forecasts for the first time are at something of a disadvantage in that they have no first-hand experience on which to draw. This does not mean that they should not attempt to plan – indeed, it is absolutely essential that they do because organisations that do not plan, fail. The lack of first-hand experience is a drawback, but there are normally other undertakings operating in the same field and much information can be obtained about them through publications such as 'Dun and Bradstreet' (*Key British Enterprises*, see Bibliography), as well as by spending money on market research. This should enable the new organisation to prepare a fairly well-informed plan of activity at least for the next year – and as those responsible for planning gain experience, their plans will improve.

Once a plan has been drawn up, it is essential that it is monitored continuously so that differences between planned and actual performance can be readily seen and corrective action taken where it is felt to be necessary. This can be achieved only if the relevant information is available at the right place and at the right time. One of the dangers of modern technology is that those responsible for making decisions receive so much information that it is sometimes difficult to 'see the wood for the trees', and important things are overlooked. It is no use telling the sales manager the number of employees in the production department, or apprising the production manager of the cost of recruiting a personnel manager, at least from the point of view of their decision-making. Nor is it useful to tell a production manager at the end of August that he failed to meet his production target in January, because the information will be too late to be of any use at all. It is here that a good management information system is invaluable to any organisation.

The personnel department has to work within organisational constraints and to the overall plan, but the resources available to it will depend, to some extent, on the personality of the personnel manager. When the budget is being prepared, each departmental manager will bid for the resources required for his or her department. The manager who is perceived to be providing good value for money and has prepared a strong case will, generally, receive a larger share of the available resources than a less well-prepared and informed manager. It is therefore essential for the well-being of the personnel department, as well as for the organisation as a whole, that the personnel manager is fully conversant with the system of budgetary control employed by the undertaking in which he or she is employed.

Having obtained an equitable share of the resources available, it is incumbent upon the personnel manager to demonstrate that the department is providing good value for its investment. To achieve this, each item of expenditure must be carefully evaluated against the best available alternative in order to demonstrate that its expenditure is being incurred because it is needed and not simply because this is the way things have always been done. Methods of developing proposals have to be continually reviewed to see whether it might be better to buy in expertise rather than supply it internally, and it is now becoming more common for personnel departments to offer their training programmes in the open market as a way of obtaining additional income for training and development.

Figure 5 illustrates a system of budgeting that provides feedback and control at every stage, both of which are essential for the system to produce information quickly and accurately. The budgetary system is an overall system of planning, within an organisation, from which is derived the master budget. This consists of statements of vital importance to organisational survival: the balance sheet, the profit and loss account, and the cash statement, each of which is detailed in this chapter and analysed in even more depth later in this book.

The balance sheet
The balance sheet provides information on the financial position of an organisation at a given date. It relates only to that date, for the position may vary significantly from day to day, which makes the date on which the balance sheet was prepared extremely important, as are the conventions that have been followed in drawing it up. Traditionally, the balance sheet has been employed largely as a historical document that shows the organisation's position at a particular point in the past and that allows relevant information to be derived from it.

Figure 5 The budgeting system

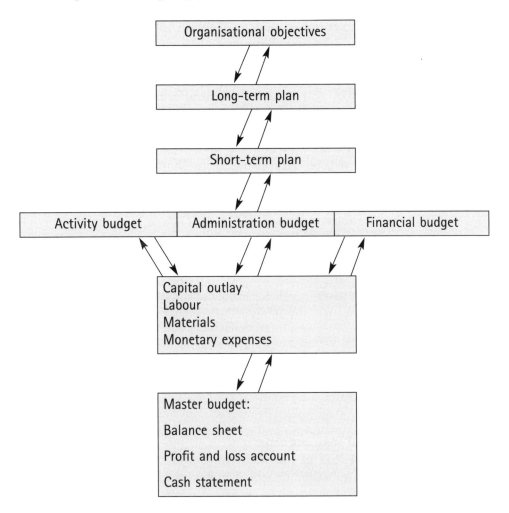

There is no reason, however, that the balance sheet should not be used – as it is more often tending to be – as a planning document, to show what an organisation will look like at some future date. The future position of the undertaking is of greater importance to those who are involved with it than what has happened in the past, although past lessons should never be forgotten.

The balance sheet is a specific sort of information system, and its two-sided form is illustrated in Example 1. Such a balance sheet, together with others, is described in greater detail in Chapter 4, but one can readily see that it could be used by the personnel manager to obtain information that might be helpful in counselling staff. The company 'X Co.' has a liquidity problem. There is a bank overdraft of £10,000 and no cash available at all, which seems to make it very difficult for 'X Co.' to pay its way. This information could be useful, for example, when advising staff on their career plans. This and much more can be deduced when the balance sheet is correctly used in conjunction with ratios, and other information, as will be demonstrated in Chapter 4.

Example 1

Balance sheet of 'X Co.' as at 31 July

	£	£		£	£
Fixed assets:			Capital	100,000	
Land and buildings	180,000		Reserves	90,000	
Plant and machinery	90,000				£190,000
Motor vehicles	25,000				
		£295,000	Loans		90,000
Current assets:			Current liabilities:		
Stock	5,000		Creditors	40,000	
Debtors	50,000		Accruals	20,000	
		55,000	Bank overdraft	10,000	
					70,000
		350,000			350,000

The profit and loss account

The profit and loss account, as its name suggests, gives information on whether or not a business, or part of it, is making a profit or loss. It is also known as a trading statement. Like the balance sheet, it can be used either as a historical document or as a planning tool. It relates to a period of time – which may be a month, a quarter, a half-year, a year, or any duration – over which the organisation wishes to measure the success or failure of its operations. The information that it provides will be greatly affected by the conventions that have been followed in its preparation, particularly in the treatment of depreciation, research and development, and goodwill. ('Goodwill' is the value over and above the book value of a business when bought, which may or may not be fully accounted for. Similarly, research and development costs may or may not be fully accounted for throughout the life of a business.)

The account is divided into two parts, the first of which records the cost of the goods that have been sold and compares it with the selling price to give the gross profit. The second part subtracts from the gross profit the fixed costs like salaries, rates, depreciation, interest charges and stationery, to arrive at the net profit.

The profit and loss account is illustrated in Example 2, but it should be borne in mind that businesses which provide a service do not normally need to calculate a gross profit. The example shows a net profit of £15,000, but we do not yet have sufficient information to know whether that is good or bad; this and other points will be explained in Chapter 5. *Opening inventory* means the stock in hand at the beginning of the period considered, and *closing inventory* means the stock in hand at the end of that period.

Example 2

Trading and profit and loss account of 'X Co.'
for the year ending 31 July

	£	£
Sales		300,000
Less Cost of goods sold:		
Opening inventory	5,000	
Add inventory purchased	180,000	
	185,000	
Deduct closing inventory	25,000	
Cost of inventory sold		160,000
Gross profit		140,000
Less Expenses:		
Wages and salaries	75,000	
Selling and distribution	10,000	
Heating and lighting	5,000	
Depreciation	15,000	
Financing charges	15,000	
Miscellaneous	5,000	
		125,000
Net profit		15,000

The cash statement

The cash statement shows the cash position of an organisation, and the balance appears in the balance sheet either under the current assets as bank/cash in hand or under the current liabilities as bank/cash overdrawn at that date. The statement can be used either for historical reporting purposes or for planning and control, and is commonly utilised in both these ways. The information it contains is of vital importance to the survival of the organisation because without money, operations would have to cease. When used as a means of planning and control the cash statement is referred to as a cash budget and prepared on a daily, weekly, monthly or quarterly basis, and is closely monitored, as described in Chapters 14 and 15.

Example 3

Cash statement of 'X Co.' for the year ending 31 July

	£	£
Opening cash in hand/(overdrawn)		30,000
Receipts from cash sales	50,000	
Receipts from credit sales	200,000	
		250,000
		280,000
Total cash available		
Deduct Payments:		
Payments for cash purchases	80,000	
Payments for credit purchases	40,000	
Wages and salaries	20,000	
Selling and distribution costs	20,000	
Heating and lighting	10,000	
Financing charges	15,000	
Miscellaneous costs	5,000	
Fixed assets purchased	100,000	
		290,000
Cash in hand/(overdrawn)		(10,000)

This is one of the most important financial management information systems, and it is almost impossible to pay too much attention to this aspect of an organisation. Example 3 shows a cash statement which indicates that the major reason for the overdraft of £10,000 is the capital expenditure of £100,000 on fixed assets during the year. (Note: figures in brackets are minus figures.)

The personnel manager is responsible for preparing the cash budget and monitoring the cash statement of his or her department. This control will normally take place on a daily basis because it is essential for the personnel manager (and indeed the whole organisation) to be constantly aware of the cash position and, where necessary, to react with the utmost speed. Many chief executives now insist that any surpluses are invested in the overnight market in order to make money.

What is a cash statement?

What is the difference between opening inventory and closing inventory? — some businesses that stock up for certain types of the year

How is the budget useful to the personnel manager?

Obtain your organisation's budget and final accounts and discuss with your personnel manager the ways in which he or she might use the information provided.

4 The balance sheet and the personnel manager

At the end of this chapter the reader should understand the structure of the balance sheet and its use in providing information to the personnel manager. The competencies that this chapter is intended to develop are those of reviewing the generation and allocation of financial resources.

The balance sheet is a statement that shows the financial position of the organisation at a specific date, and like all statements its accuracy is dependent on the information system employed to compile it. If the information on which it is based is inaccurate, the balance sheet will be inaccurate. This illustrates how critical a good management information system is in the effective running of an organisation. In drawing up a balance sheet it is necessary to follow accounting conventions, which will be explored as we work through some illustrations.

Example 4
An entrepreneur has £120,000 with which to start a business, and pays it into the business's bank account. The balance sheet then shows:

Business balance sheet as at day 1

	£		£
Uses:		Sources:	
Bank	120,000	Capital	120,000

The balance sheet shows that £120,000 has been put into the business by the owner and that at the time of the balance sheet it was all in the bank. Any resource put into a business by the owner(s) becomes part of the capital, and all sources of finance are shown on the right-hand side of the two-sided balance sheet. The uses of finance, including money in the bank, are shown on the left-hand side. Every balance sheet uses these principles, and if they are broken down item by item, a great deal of the confusion that often surrounds them can readily be overcome.

Example 5
Premises are required for the business, and enquiries lead to the purchase of a small lock-up shop for £50,000 on day 2. The shop is paid for and the balance sheet becomes:

Business balance sheet as at day 2

	£		£
Uses:		Sources:	
Premises	50,000	Capital	120,000
Bank	70,000		
	120,000		120,000

No new resources have been put into the business by the owner, nor have any resources been withdrawn, which leaves the capital unchanged; and because no other resources have been provided, there is no change on the 'Sources' side of the balance sheet. On the 'Uses' side, the money has been taken from the bank and invested in the premises, as reflected in the new balance sheet.

Example 6
The premises having been obtained, the business now requires inventory to sell in order to start trading: £1,000 of goods are purchased for cash on day 3. This transaction is shown in the balance sheet as:

Business balance sheet as at day 3

	£		£
Uses:		Source:	
Premises	50,000	Capital	120,000
Inventory/stock	1,000		
Bank	69,000		
	120,000		120,000

The Sources side of the balance sheet remains unchanged, but there has been a further change of Use – £1,000 has been taken from the bank to purchase inventory (which may also be referred to as 'stock') consisting of items held by the business for resale in order to earn a profit.

Example 7
Inventory that cost £100 is sold for £100 cash on day 6 to attract people into the shop. The balance sheet then shows:

Business balance sheet as at day 6

Uses:	£	Sources:	£
Premises	50,000	Capital	120,000
Inventory/stock	900		
Bank	69,100		
	120,000		120,000

Once again the Sources side of the balance sheet remains unchanged but the inventory is reduced by the £100 that has been sold and the bank increased by the £100 that has been received from the sale.

Example 8
On day 8 the business is really ready for action, and inventory that cost £800 is sold for £1,600 cash. The balance sheet now shows:

Business balance sheet as at day 8

Uses:	£	Sources:	£
Premises	50,000	Capital	120,000
Inventory/stock	100	Reserves:	
Bank	70,700	Retained profit	800
	120,800		120,800

The Sources side of the balance sheet is increased by the profit on the sale of £800, which is shown under the reserves. This is balanced by the reduction in inventory of £800 and the increased bank balance of £1,600, which illustrates the fact that all the resources a business receives must be accounted for, whatever their nature, and explains why the balance sheet should always balance. The premises remain unchanged at £50,000.

Example 9
The business is now in full stride, and on day 9 further inventory is purchased for £3,000, of which £2,000 is in cash and £1,000 is credit.

Business balance sheet as at day 9

Uses:		£	Sources:		£
	Premises	50,000	Capital		£120,000
	Inventory/stock	3,100	Reserves:		
			Retained profit		800
	Bank	68,700	Creditor		1,000
		121,800			121,800

A new item appears on the Sources side of the balance sheet, called Creditor, of £1,000. Creditors are people who are owed money by the business for goods or services they have provided. This item is balanced by an increase of £3,000 in the inventory and a reduction in the bank balance of £2,000; no other changes take place in the balance sheet. It is interesting to note that the reserves are £800 but the bank balance is £68,700. Reserves are not normally equal to cash.

Example 10
Business is booming. To encourage it, credit is offered to reliable customers, and on day 10 inventory that cost £1,800 is sold for £3,600. The sales consist of £600 for cash and £3,000 on credit. The balance sheet now shows:

Business balance sheet as at day 10

Uses:	£	Sources:	£
Premises	50,000	Capital	120,000
Inventory	1,300	Reserves:	
Debtors	3,000	Retained profit	2,600
Bank	69,300	Creditor	1,000
	123,600		123,600

The capital and creditor on the Sources side remain unchanged, whereas the reserves are increased by the profit of £1,800 to £2,600, although the bank balance is £69,300. Reserves do *not* represent cash. On the Uses side, inventory is reduced by the £1,800 that has been sold, to £1,300; the bank balance is increased by the £600 received from the sale, to £69,300; and debtors of £3,000 for the credit sales appear. (People who owe money to the business for goods or services received are its debtors.)

Example 11
The business receives £1,200 that it is owed by some of its debtors and pays what is owed to its suppliers on day 11. The balance sheet shows:

	£			£
Business balance sheet as at day 11				
Uses:		Sources:		
Premises	50,000	Capital		120,000
Inventory	1,300	Reserves:		
Debtors	1,800	Retained Profit	2,600	
Bank	69,500			
	122,600			122,600

The only change on the Sources side is the disappearance of the creditor for £1,000 because payment has been made. On the Uses side, the debtors are reduced by the £1,200 that they have paid and the bank balance is increased by £200 (£1,200 − £1,000); the premises and inventory remain unchanged.

You will have noticed that nothing that happens to a business can ever have only a single impact on the balance sheet. If it did, the balance sheet would never balance and would serve no useful purpose. As has already been noted, the balance sheet, by its very nature, should always balance, and so each transaction that takes place must affect more than one aspect of it. Transactions may have seven impacts or more but never just a single one, and this is the basis of the double-entry system of book-keeping that has been employed since the time of the Phoenicians. When we accountants see a good thing, we know how to cherish it!

Some conventions have been followed in constructing the balance sheets, and these should be explained in a little more detail. The Sources and Uses sides are each arranged in order of permanence, so that the most permanent item is at the top and the least permanent at the bottom. The Uses are divided into *fixed*, which are retained in the business to earn profits, like land and buildings, and *current*, which are consumed in order to earn profits, like inventory and money. The sources are allocated between *permanent*, consisting of capital and reserves, *long-term*, consisting of loans, and *current*, which includes creditors. The balance sheet in Example 10 takes the following form when these conventions are emphasised:

Example 10, Redrawn 1

Business balance sheet as at day 10

	£	£		£
Uses:			Sources:	
Fixed uses:			Capital	120,000
Premises		50,000	Reserves:	
Fixtures/fittings			Retained profit	2,600
Motor vehicles			Loans	
			Current sources:	
Current uses:			Creditor	1,000
Inventory	1,300			
Debtors	3,000			
Bank	69,300	73,600		
		123,600		123,600

These divisions between fixed and current uses and between permanent, long-term and current sources become important when we start to look at the interpretation of financial information by the personnel manager.

Another convention that is normally followed is for Sources to be called 'liabilities'. This is because everything on that side is technically held by the business on somebody else's behalf. The capital and reserves belong to the owner(s) of the business, the loans consist of money which belongs to the lenders, and creditors are the people who supplied the credit, so that everything on that side is a liability of the undertaking.

The Uses are called 'assets' because they are owned by the business. The premises, inventory and bank balance are all owned by the business, and the debtors are obliged to pay the business, so that their debt is owned by it. Using this new but more usually accepted terminology, the balance sheet now becomes:

Example 10, Redrawn 2

Business balance sheet as at day 10

	£	£		£
Assets			*Liabilities*	
Fixed assests:			Capital	120,000
Premises	50,000		Reserves:	
Fixtures/fittings			Retained profit	2,600
Motor vehicles	———		Loans	
		£50,000	Current liabilities:	
Current assets:			Creditor	1,000
Inventory	1,300		Accruals	
Debtors	3,000			
Bank	69,300			
		73,600		———
		123,600		123,600

The fixtures and fittings and motor vehicles have been included as examples of fixed assets, and the loans are an example of a long-term liability just as the accruals are of a short-term liability, although nothing is yet shown against them. (Accruals are sums due to be paid for items such as rent, rates and electricity.) Note that the second column of figures under *Assets* are cumulative totals.

The balance sheets presented here have so far been in the two-sided form because that facilitates the explanation, but most organisations publish their balance sheets in a vertical form, so we will redraw the above balance sheet in that form to illustrate the approach.

Organisations prefer to publish the balance sheet in the vertical (or, as it is sometimes called, the narrative) form because they believe it to be easier for a lay person to understand than the two-sided form. Items considered to be important – like the net current assets (working capital) and net assets employed (net capital employed) – are highlighted and can be further explored should the need arise. This will be further outlined in Chapter 7 when we look at the interpretation of financial information.

When an organisation turns itself into a limited company, the major impact in the balance sheet is under the 'Capital' heading. If our example business decided, in its formation documentation, that it would take upon itself the authority to

Example 10, Redrawn 3

Business balance sheet as at day 10

	£	£
Fixed assets:		
Premises	50,000	
Fixtures and fittings		
Motor vehicles	———	
		£50,000
Current assets:		
Inventory	1,300	
Debtors	3,000	
Bank	69,300	
	73,600	
Less Current liabilities:		
Creditors	1,000	
Accruals		
Net current assets (working capital)	———	72,600
Net assets employed (net capital employed)		122,600
Financed by:		
Capital	120,000	
Reserves	2,600	
Owner's equity		122,600
		122,600

issue 400,000 shares of £1.00 each, and in fact issued 122,600 shares to the owner in return for the owner's equity, then the net assets employed (net capital employed) would be exactly as illustrated above, and total £122,600, but the 'Financed by' section becomes:

Financed by:	
Authorised capital:	
400,000 shares of £1.00 each	£400,000
Issued capital:	
122,600 shares of £1.00 each	£122,600
Reserves	
Owner's equity	£122,600
Loans	
	£122,600

The share capital comprising 122,600 shares at £1.00 has replaced the original owner's equity, which consisted of capital and reserves. This is to compensate the owner for the work that has to be carried out in starting up a business.

The following questions are for you to attempt before you check against the sample answers provided at the back of the book.

Exercise 1
Sacha has inherited £60,000 and intends to use it to fulfil a lifelong dream of setting up in business. On 5 June the money is paid into the business bank account. Draw up the balance sheet as at 5 June.

Exercise 2
On 6 June Sacha obtains premises for £80,000, of which £40,000 is paid from the business bank account by cash and the other £40,000 is borrowed. Draw up the balance sheet as at 6 June.

Exercise 3
On 7 June fixtures and fittings of £8,000 are bought for cash. A small van that has been in Sacha's possession, worth £1,500, is brought into the business. Draw up the balance sheet as at 7 June.

Exercise 4
The business is now ready, so on 8 June Sacha buys inventory for £30,000, of which £20,000 is a credit purchase and the balance is paid in cash. Draw up the balance sheet as at 8 June.

Exercise 5
Sacha sells inventory that cost £20,000 for £60,000 on 9 June: £50,000 of the sales were on credit and the balance for cash. Draw up the balance sheet as at 9 June.

Exercise 6
The business is doing so well that on 10 June Sacha decides to turn it into a limited company, and issues 203,000 shares at 50p for the owner's equity. Draw up the balance sheet to show how it would appear after this transaction, in both the two-sided and vertical forms.

In every case the balance sheets show the financial position of the business at a particular date, and have been drawn up after the transactions have occurred, and so constitute historical documents. There is no reason that they should not be used as planning tools, showing the position it is planned for the business to be in at some specific future date. This will be further discussed in Chapter 14.

We have now together gone through a series of balance sheets, and (we hope) you have completed some exercises that should afford you a good understanding of how a balance sheet is made up and of those items that would be of particular interest to a personnel manager. A more detailed interpretation of the information the balance sheet contains (and its relevance to personnel managers) appears in Chapter 7, where the accounts of Sainsbury's are analysed.

What is capital?

What are reserves?

What is the purpose of working capital?

Why would the personnel manager be concerned about a high level of debtors?

What does net capital employed represent?

What is authorised capital?

Study your organisation's balance sheet. Compare the total reserves with the bank and cash figures. Explain why they differ.

5 The trading and profit and loss account and the personnel manager

At the end of this chapter the reader should understand the profit and loss account and cash statement and their use in providing information to the personnel manager. The competencies that this chapter is intended to develop are those of reviewing the generation and allocation of financial resources.

We have seen from the previous chapter that it is possible to draw up a fresh balance sheet after every transaction that takes place in an organisation, but in the light of the number of transactions that take place it would become extremely cumbersome to do so. To overcome the problem we have to devise some method of presenting transactions collectively in a format that is helpful to those who need the information as well as being meaningful in financial terms. This is achieved through the trading and profit and loss account.

The balance sheet shows the position of the business at a specific date in the past or at a planned future date. The trading and profit and loss account (sometimes referred to as the income statement) shows the results of an organisation's activities over a period of time which may be a week, a month, several months, or a year, either as planned for or as has occurred in the past. In preparing the trading and profit and loss account several accounting principles have to be observed. The principles have to be observed to ensure that such accounts are prepared on a consistent basis from one year to the next. This makes them more useful to the personnel manager and others when they compare the results of several trading periods to ascertain the success or otherwise of the undertaking.

ACCOUNTING PRINCIPLES

The matching principle

This ensures that each accounting period stands alone and collects all the earnings and expenses which relate to it. There is a danger that when transactions overlap two accounting periods they will be counted twice – once in each period – or missed altogether. The matching principle helps to prevent this.

For example, assume that the profit and loss account is drawn up for the year from 1 January to 31 December, and that business rates of £1,000 are paid on 1 October for the six months to 31 March. Then the three months until 31 December will belong in one profit and loss account and the three months until 31 March will belong in the next. This is extremely important if the accounts are to be accurate enough to enable them to be used for purposes of comparison as well as recording the correct profit or loss.

A model of the organisation through time would be like Figure 6. If we did not have to manage the business, or pay taxes, or go on living ourselves, we would be able to wait until the end of the organisation's life before calculating the profit or loss that had been made. Unfortunately this is not possible, so each period's profit or loss has to be calculated. It is essential to ensure that all amounts which relate to the specified period are included and that any which relate to any other period are excluded. Achieving this happy result causes many problems in the preparation of financial information.

Figure 6 Organisational accounting through time

Start	Year 1	Year 2	Year 3	Year 4	Year 5	Year 6	Year 99	End
	Profit	Profit	Profit	Profit	Profit	Profit	Profit	Profit
	Loss	Loss	Loss	Loss	Loss	Loss	Loss	Loss
Balance sheet	Balance sheet	Balance sheet	Balance sheet	Balance sheet	Balance sheet	Balance sheet	Balance sheet	Balance sheet

The principle of consistency

This helps in comparing performance in one financial period with that in another. If the methods employed when preparing the profit and loss accounts keep changing, comparison becomes impossible, so a decision must be made on how each item is to be dealt with. That method must continue in use unless there is a very good reason for changing it.

An example is the way an organisation treats the charge for the use of fixed assets in the profit and loss account. Because of their nature, most fixed assets are expensive and last a long time. It would be unfair if one accounting period were charged for the whole cost of a fixed asset so that the other periods had free use of it. The period in which the asset was bought would show a loss and the other periods a profit – for example:

	£	£
Sales	80,000	
Cost of sales	20,000	
Gross profit		60,000
Expenses	40,000	
New fixed asset	100,000	
		140,000
Net loss		(80,000)

In the next period, if the organisation just happened to achieve exactly the same performance, the accounts would show:

	£
Sales	80,000
Cost of sales	20,000
Gross profit	60,000
Expenses	40,000
Net profit	20,000

In order to avoid these wide fluctuations in profit there is a means of charging a 'rent' for fixed assets, which we call depreciation. There are several ways of calculating the charge for depreciation. All are perfectly acceptable, but the one that is most commonly used is the straight-line approach, which charges the same sum for the use of each specific asset over its life. To calculate the period charge for depreciation, three pieces of information are required – cost, life, and scrap value.

If we have an asset that costs £101,000 which we estimate will last for ten years and have a residual scrap value of £1,000, then the charge for depreciation is given by:

$$\frac{\text{Cost} - \text{Scrap}}{\text{Life}} \quad = \quad \frac{£101,000 - £1,000}{10 \text{ years}}$$

$$= \quad \frac{£100,000}{10 \text{ years}} \quad = \quad £10,000 \text{ p.a.}$$

This will make the profit in our example:

	£	£
Sales	80,000	
Cost of sales	20,000	
Gross profit		60,000
Expenses	40,000	
Depreciation	10,000	
		50,000
Net profit		10,000

This irons out the fluctuations in profit and facilitates comparison of performance.

The principle of conservatism

Accountants are by nature pessimistic. We feel it is better to look on the dark side and be surprised if things turn out better than expected than to look on the bright side and be surprised if things turn out worse than expected. This is the principle of conservatism, under which we always anticipate losses but never profits. It is clearly demonstrated in the way in which inventory is valued.

Inventory is always valued at the lower of cost or current market value. If an item has been purchased for £6,000 and its market value goes up to £8,000, it is valued in the accounts at £6,000. However, if its market value goes down to £4,000, it is valued in the accounts at £4,000.

The principle of differentiating between capital and revenue items

Capital transactions involve fixed assets and affect the balance sheet, so that if we buy new machinery, it appears under fixed assets in the balance sheet and the bank balance is reduced by the same amount. There is, at the time, no impact on the profit and loss account, but there will be at some later date, through the charge for depreciation.

Revenue transactions relate to running expenses like heating and lighting, rent and rates, wages and salaries, which have a direct impact on the profit and loss account but no direct effect on the balance sheet. They will, however, later affect the retained profit under the reserves.

PROFIT

Now that we have discussed the principles involved in the preparation of the trading and profit and loss account, let us see if we can decide what profit is and why it so often differs from cash. Profit may roughly be described as *the earnings of the period concerned, whether or not they have been received, minus the expenses of the same period, whether or not they have been paid.*

To take this a little further, profit may be illustrated as:

	£	£
Sales:		
Credit	80,000	
Cash	20,000	
		100,000
Expenses:		
Credit	10,000	
Cash	50,000	
		60,000
Profit		40,000

The earnings are £100,000 and the expenses £60,000, giving a profit of £40,000 – but what has been the effect on the bank balance? The bank balance has not, as we might have expected, been increased by the profit of £40,000 but reduced by £30,000. This is because the actual amounts of money have been:

	£
Payments for expenses	50,000
Receipts from sales	20,000
Net cash outflow	30,000

The other transactions have involved credit, not cash. This shows that a profit of £40,000 has resulted in a cash reduction of £30,000, which highlights the important difference between profitability and liquidity, and helps to explain why so many profitable companies fail because they do not have the means to pay their way.

Let us look more closely at the trading and profit and loss account. We will use the illustration given in Example 2, on page 25. The statement could have been prepared historically on 15 October, or it could have been devised as a planning document and prepared on 1 May. Whatever its purposes, the principles on which it is prepared are exactly the same, To reinforce the point we will go through the entries item by item.

Sales £300,000
This figure represents the total sales for the year and it is included whether or not any money has been received. Money received late on account of last year's sales would be excluded from this year's figure.

Opening inventory £5,000
This is the stock that was left over, unsold, at the end of the previous trading period. It is valued at cost or current market value, whichever is the lower.

Inventory purchased £180,000
This is the total purchases of stock for the year and is included whether or not the money has been paid. Money paid late on account of last year's purchases would be excluded from the figure.

Closing inventory £25,000

This is the stock that has not been sold and is valued at the lower of cost or current market value.

Wages and salaries £75,000

This is the total that should have been paid during the year, taken from the wage records. Any wages that are due but unpaid would be included in this figure.

Selling and distribution £10,000

This includes all the expenses that have been incurred during the year, whether they have been paid or not.

Heating and lighting £5,000

This represents the electricity, oil, gas, coal, etc, that has been consumed during the year. Some apportionment may be necessary to ensure that only the expenses that relate to the year are borne by the year. It can be obtained from accounts received and metered readings.

Depreciation £15,000

This is the charge decided upon for the use of the fixed assets, as described under the principle of consistency. It is purely an apportionment of expenses and does not involve money.

Financing charges £15,000

This is the total of the costs incurred in raising loans and the interest paid on them. It does not include the repayment of loans (ie of the principal of a loan), which is a balance-sheet item (a capital transaction).

Miscellaneous £5,000

This represents the total of a whole series of sundry expenses, including telephone, postage, writing materials, refreshments and office cleaning.

Net profit £15,000

This is the figure that, once it has been adjusted for things like taxation, will appear in the balance sheet under Reserves.

ADDED VALUE

So far we have discussed gross and net profit and you should have some understanding of the concepts involved. There is, however, an additional concept to which businesses and their owners attach great importance. This is 'added value', which illustrates how much as organisation is able to mark up on top of the costs incurred when arriving at the selling price of a product. The concept has been developed to such an extent that it is one of the factors used when assessing the strength of a company.

Added value is calculated in the following way:

Sales turnover + Other income = Gross income

Gross income − Bought-out costs = Added value

Added value − Wage costs = Net profit before tax

Applying this to Example 2, page 25, we have:

		£
Sales turnover		300,000
Less Materials	160,000	
Selling	10,000	
Heating	5,000	
Finance	15,000	
Miscellaneous	5,000	
		195,000
Added value		£105,000

The added value then goes to meet wage costs and depreciation. If there is any left when these costs have been met, it becomes profit.

The trading and profit and loss account – and its relevance to the personal manager as an aid to decision-making – is explored more fully in Chapter 7 through the medium of the accounts of Sainsbury's.

We have illustrated two financial statements: one which provides information about the position of a business at a given date – the balance sheet – and another which shows the results of a period of activity in terms of profit – the trading and profit and loss account (or income statement). We will now concentrate on the cash statement, which shows what has happened to the money in the organisation and relates to the bank/cash-in-hand or overdrawn figure in the balance sheet, and which is of great importance to the personnel manager because it shows whether or not there is sufficient money for the survival of the undertaking.

As is the case with the balance sheet and trading and profit and loss account, this statement can be prepared either for planning purposes or as a historical document to show the results of past activities. When it is prepared for planning purposes on a daily, weekly or monthly basis, the cash statement becomes the *cash budget*, which is dealt with in detail in Chapter 14. In preparing the statement for past activities we have to concentrate on the movements of money rather than on the transactions that have taken place. For example, the sales of £300,000 in Example 2 on page 25 may consist of £200,000 cash and £100,000 credit, and £60,000 cash could additionally have been received from credit sales in the previous year ending 31 July. Cash received would therefore be £260,000 and not the £300,000 shown as sales. We need to look at each entry in Example 2 and arrive at its cash equivalent in order for the cash statement to be prepared. This will further emphasise the difference between profitability and liquidity.

Opening stock of finished goods
No cash movement.

Add inventory purchased
This depends on what has been paid. It could be that £150,000 was for cash and £30,000 on credit, but a further £50,000 could have been paid for previously purchased items so that the payment would be £200,000 (£150,000 + £50,000) and not the £180,000 shown.

Less closing inventory
No cash movement.

Wages and salaries
These would all be paid: £75,000.

Selling and distribution
There could be some outstanding payments, say £3,000, and £1,500 could have been paid for the previous year's outstanding, making the cash movement £8,500 (£10,000 – £3,000 + £1,500).

Heating and lighting
Some of these accounts could be waiting to be paid – say £4,000 – and £3,000 relating to last year could have been paid. This would make the cash £4,000 (£5,000 – £4,000 + £3,000).

Depreciation
No cash movement. Depreciation is purely an apportionment of costs and does not increase cash movements.

Financing charges
This depends on what has been paid. If they have all been paid, together with £3,000 from the previous year, the cash movement would be £18,000.

Miscellaneous
There is possibly £1,000 due to be paid for last year's expense, making the cash movement £6,000.

There could well be other items that are not shown in this profit and loss account which would affect the cash balance. For example, the purchase of a new fixed asset, like machinery, for £80,000 would have a big impact. And had the owner drawn any money from the business for his or her own purpose, that would have affected the cash but might well not have been included in salaries. If the owner is not paid a salary, then any money he or she draws is treated as if the owner were reclaiming some of the resources that were due from the business. On the other hand, if the owner is paid a salary for working in the business, it is shown under salaries and not treated as drawings.

The historical cash statement drawn up on the above figures, assuming the opening balance was £2,000, becomes Example 12.

Example 12

Cash statement of 'X Co.' for the year ending 31 July

	£	£
Opening balance in hand/(overdrawn)		2,0000
Add Receipts from cash sales		200,000
Add Receipts from previous credit sales		60,000
Total cash available		262,000
Less Cash payments:		
Goods purchased for cash	150,000	
Add payments for previous credit purchases	50,000	
Wages and salaries	75,000	
Selling and distribution	8,500	
Heating and lighting	4,000	
Finance charges	18,000	
Miscellaneous	6,000	
		311,500
Closing cash in hand (overdrawn)		(49,500)

The result of the activities has been a profit of £15,000. But at the same time there has been a cash outflow of £51,500 (ie £311,500 − £260,000) which, after deducting the opening balance of £2,000, leaves an overdraft of £49,500 − once again emphasising that profitability is by no means the same thing as liquidity.

Bear in mind that no matter how large or small an organisation is or whether it is in the public or the private sector, exactly the same principles are employed when the cash statement is prepared. The cash statement of a large manufacturing concern would include the items illustrated in Example 13.

Example 13

	£	£
	(000)	(000)
Opening balance	40	
Add Receipts:		
Money from trading	40,000	
Investment receipts	100	
		40,140
Less Payments:		
Raw materials	1,020	
Fuel and light	80	
Factory wages	22,144	
Administrative salaries	12,256	
Carriage outwards	250	
Business rate	2,300	
General office expenses	80	
Repairs	59	
Financing costs	121	
		38,310
Closing balance in hand		1,830

Individual departments within an organisation can also have their own cash statements, since it is necessary for each manager to control his or her departmental cash situation. This is discussed in detail in Chapter 13, but the statement of a typical personnel department would like something like Example 14.

Example 14

Personnel department cash statement

	£	£
	(000)	(000)
Opening balance	£20	
Share of organisational budget	180	
Externally-provided training courses	90	
Inter-departmental training charges	40	
		330
Payments:		
Salaries	190	
Recruitment costs	60	
Training costs	60	
Heat and light	5	
Telephone, postage	8	
Service charge	7	
		330
Balance		

The following exercises relate to Chapters 4 and 5, and are for you to attempt before comparing your answers with the sample solutions that appear at the end of the book.

Exercise 7

Thomas has £5,000 with which to make a living and decides to become a market-stallholder. He buys a pair of scales that cost £586, will last for an estimated six years and have a scrap value of £40, and a market stall on wheels that cost £1,140, will last an estimated four years and have a scrap value of £100. During his first four weeks' trading he buys second-grade fruit out of his original £5,000 for £2,600. At the end of the four weeks he has sold £4,240-worth of goods. He has £3,800 left out of this after paying out:

	£
Rent of yard	120 (£40 per week)
Weekend help	180
Obstruction fines	140

At the end of the period he owes £40 rent and has fruit left unsold which cost £240. He considers half the fruit still to be saleable. Calculate the profit for the period, the cash statement and the balance sheet at the end.

Exercise 8

At the start of his second four weeks' operations Thomas is in the following position:

	£
Inventory of saleable fruit costing	120
Cash in hand	4,474
One week's rent owing	40
A stall and a pair of scales	1,699

In the second four weeks he buys £3,900-worth of fruit for cash. He decides, after consulting his accountant, that he should spend £400 on household expenses. He takes out a loss-of-profits insurance policy at the beginning of the period, payable in advance, at an annual premium of £208. Other cash transactions during the four weeks are:

	£
Rent	120 (three weeks)
Fines	260
Help	180
Cash takings	5,000

Closing value of inventory at cost is £500, half of which is in good condition and half of which he thinks will fetch only £150 (three tenths of cost). What are his profit for the period, his cash balance and his financial position at the end of the second period? He finds he needs more to cover household costs. Can he afford it?

Exercise 9

Thomas's position at the start of the third four weeks is:

	£
Two weeks' rent owing	80
Insurance pre-paid	192
Inventory of fruit	400
Cash in hand	4,406
A pair of scales and the stall	1,672

During the four weeks he buys fruit for £5,000 cash and feels that he can increase his household expenditure to £600. He does so and retains the balance of the money in the business. Other payments and receipts during the four weeks are:

	£
Rent	200 (five weeks)
Fines (one prosecution is pending: the fine is expected to be £300)	nil
Weekend help	180
Cash takings for the month	6,000

On the last day of the period he purchases a delivery van for £5,100 and sells his stall for £800. The value of his closing inventory is £600 at cost price. What is Thomas's profit for the period? Is there a profit or a loss on the sale of the stall? What is his financial position at the end of the period?

Exercise 10
Thomas starts his fourth four weeks with:

	£
Cash in hand	126
Provision for parking fine	300
Rent owing	40
Fruit unsold	600
Insurance pre-paid	176
Van	5,100
Scales	565

He senses that he is running into a cash-flow problem but his household costs are rising and so he increases the allocation to £650. The magistrates fine him £140 for the outstanding case of obstruction, and he decides to expand his business by starting a delivery round on the first day of the period, selling fresh vegetables with the fruit. He expects to keep the van for three years and then sell it for £810. His suppliers agree to let him open a credit account, and the following transactions take place during the fourth four weeks:

	£
Total cash purchases	3,500
Total purchases on credit	3,000
Cash takings	6,100
Sales on credit to families whom he feels he can trust and who have promised to pay him next month	400
Inventory of fruit and vegetables at the end of the period at market value	1,700

His other cash transactions during the four weeks are:

	£
Vehicle running expenses	100
Annual vehicle license	130
Rent paid	160
Weekend help	180
Payments to creditors	1,800

What is Thomas's profit for the period? What is his financial position at the end of the period? Does it accurately represent the worth of the business?

How do you calculate profit?

How do you calculate liquidity?

What do you understand by added value?

What is gross profit?

What is net profit?

What is more important to the personnel manager – cash or profit?

Draw up a cash statement for your department and discuss its content with an accountant to reinforce your learning.

6 The manufacturing account and the personnel department

At the end of this chapter the reader should understand the preparation of the manufacturing account and its use to the personnel manager as a source of information. The management competence that this chapter is intended to develop is that of reviewing the generation and allocation of financial resources.

Organisations that manufacture their own goods for sale require an additional financial statement to provide information on the manufacturing cost of the goods that are being made. This helps to ensure that the manufacturing manager is able to maintain control over his or her operation and that the correct information is provided to facilitate good decision-making. The manufacturing account comes before the trading and profit and loss account, and collects together all the costs of manufacture. These are transferred to the trading and profit and loss account in the 'Cost of goods sold' section, where it replaces 'Inventory purchased'. We shall explore this more fully as we work through Example 16, but it is important to remember that the manufacturing account is part of the management information system and can either be prepared historically or be used as a planning tool for the future.

The manufacturing account contains a great deal of information about wages and salaries, both direct and indirect, that is of interest to the personnel department. Direct wages relate to those people who are directly involved in the manufacturing process – ie those who actually make something. Indirect wages relate to those who are not actually producing anything – like supervisors, cleaners and maintenance people.

Example 15

Manufacturing account of Makes Co. for the year ending 30 June

	£	£
Opening inventory of raw materials	40,000	
Add Raw materials purchased	810,000	
	850,000	
Deduct Closing inventory of raw materials		
Raw materials consumed	60,000	790,000
Direct manufacturing wages		1,410,000
Direct expenses		10,000
Prime/direct cost of goods made		2,210,000
Add Indirect factory expenses/overheads:		
Salaries and wages	70,000	
Materials	30,000	
Heating and lighting	40,000	
Rent and rates	60,000	
Depreciation	90,000	
		290,000
Total manufacturing costs		2,500,000
Add Opening work in progress		10,000
		2,510,000
Deduct Closing work in progress		20,000
Cost of finished goods made		2,490,000

Example 15 shows a manufacturing account, which contains useful information for management. It can be made even more useful if it is broken down into the cost per unit produced, as we will see in Chapter 11. The way in which the manufacturing account fits in with the trading and profit and loss accounts will be demonstrated later, but in order to clarify the situation let us first look at each item in the manufacturing account in turn.

Opening inventory of raw materials
The raw materials that are available to be used at the beginning of the financial period. They are valued at the lower of cost or current market value.

Raw materials purchased
The raw materials purchased during the financial period under review. They need not necessarily have been paid for.

Closing inventory of raw materials
The raw materials that are left unused at the end of the financial period. They become the opening stock of raw

materials for the new period and are valued at the lower of cost or current market value.

Raw materials consumed
The raw materials that have actually been used in the manufacturing process.

Direct manufacturing wages
The wages of the people who are directly involved in making the product. It includes the machine operators but excludes supervisors and packers.

Direct expenses
Expenses that can be identified with a particular product, and which increase as the number of units produced increases. An example would be the amount of power used by one individual machine making a single product. There are often no direct expenses in a manufacturing concern.

Indirect factory expenses/overheads
Expenses that are not identified with a particular product and generally remain fixed irrespective of the number of items that are produced. It is often difficult to arrive at the total to be charged to the manufacturing account, as opposed to the trading and profit and loss account. For example, a small manufacturing concern may have one rates bill for the whole site, and then have to apportion it between the manufacturing and non-manufacturing areas.

Salaries and wages
The remuneration paid to the factory manager, supervisors, cleaners and others whose time is spent in the manufacturing area.

Materials
The cost of materials used in the area that do not go directly into the product. They include such things as cleaning materials, packaging and general-issue items like screws.

Heating and lighting

The cost of heating and lighting the factory or workshop area. If there is one bill for the whole premises, some apportionment between the manufacturing and non-manufacturing areas will be necessary.

Rent and rates

The cost of rent and rates relating to the factory or workshop. Some apportionment will be necessary between the manufacturing and non-manufacturing areas if they are not billed separately.

Depreciation

The charge for the use of machinery, equipment, buildings and other fixed assets in the manufacturing area.

Total manufacturing costs

The total cost, collected together in the manufacturing account, of all the items that have been produced.

The relationship of the manufacturing account to the trading and profit and loss accounts can be illustrated as in Example 16:

Example 16

Trading and profit and loss account of Makes Co. for the year ending 30 June

	£	£
Sales		7,600,000
Less Cost of goods sold:		
Opening inventory of finished goods	40,000	
Add Cost of goods manufactured (from	2,490,000	
the manufacturing account)	2,530,000	
D*educt* closing inventory of finished goods	30,000	
Cost of finished goods sold		2,500,000
Gross profit		£5,100,000

This is the end of the trading account. We then go on to the profit and loss account section:

	£	£
Gross profit		£5,100,000
Less Expenses:		
Wages and salaries	3,750,000	
Selling and distribution	250,000	
Heating and lighting	40,000	
Depreciation	120,000	
Financing charges	65,000	
Miscellaneous	15,000	
		4,240,000
Net profit before tax		860,000

There would then be deductions for tax but the amount would depend on the current tax legislation, which changes every year, and is therefore beyond the scope of this book.

The manufacturing account is used to ensure that the costs of manufacturing are properly controlled and that wastage is kept to a minimum. Correctly and promptly prepared accounts ensure that management is fully conversant with the current situation and able to take corrective action quickly when it proves to be necessary. If, for example, the production manager has evidence that raw material costs are escalating because of theft, he or she would liaise with the personnel manager to ensure that the correct procedures were being followed.

It may be that the organisation finds that the demand for its manufactured product is price-sensitive and that a competitor is selling an equivalent item more cheaply. This will cause market share to be lost so that management will have to decide on how to combat the threat. The manufacturing account should provide sufficient detail for the cost of each item manufactured to be calculated. Comparison with the competitor's selling-price of the product will indicate to the management the courses of action that are open to it. Where the competitor's price is higher than the manufacturing cost it might be possible to reduce the selling-price in order to reclaim lost market share. If, on the other hand, the manufacturing cost is higher than the competitor's selling-price, then management has a major problem to resolve.

The selling-price could be reduced below the cost price in

the hope of recovering market share and possibly forcing the competitor out of business, but this is an extremely high-risk strategy and could not be pursued for a long period unless the organisation is financially strong. A second option would be to investigate ways of reducing manufacturing costs so that the selling-price could be brought down.

The personnel manager might well be closely involved in this process since a common way of controlling costs is by reducing staff numbers and providing counselling for those made redundant. In the event that neither of these strategies is practicable, a search may be made for a new product or products into which it might be worth diversifying. The last resort would be to endeavour to sell the organisation as a going concern before it was forced into liquidation.

Example 15 shows that the cost of goods made was £2,490,000. If that cost was for manufacturing 800,000 units, the cost per unit would be:

$$£2,490,000 \div 800,000 = £3.1125$$

A competitor coming to the market with a similar product selling at £10 would not, under normal circumstances, present a major threat. On the other hand one coming into the market at £5 would be a major problem particularly as the product is at present selling for £9.46 (assuming sales of 803,382 units to achieve the sales value of £7,600,000 shown in the accounts).

How is the manufacturing account of use to the personnel department?

What are direct expenses?

What is prime cost?

Why is the manufacturing account an aid to pricing?

How does the manufacturing account link with the trading account?

Obtain the manufacturing account of two organisations and compare the information provided. Do they appear to have been prepared on the same basis? Which do you consider to be the easier to understand?

7 The interpretation and use of financial information for personnel

At the end of this chapter the reader should understand the purpose of ratios and their application in assessing the performance of organisations from the point of view of the personnel manager. The management competencies that this chapter is intended to develop are those of evaluating proposals for expenditure and controlling expenditure against budget.

In the preceding chapters we have investigated the financial information provided by the management information system and noted the danger of information's being received too late to be useful. Assuming that the organisation has ensured that the correct information is reaching the right person quickly enough to be used, we will look at some of the ratios that help personnel make better use of the information in planning and control.

The ratios break down into three main areas: profitability, liquidity, and efficiency or activity. We will investigate each in turn, using the account of 'Trader Co.'.

Example 17

Trading and profit and loss account of Trader Co. for the year ending 31 August

	£	£
Sales		960,000
Less Cost of goods sold:		
Opening inventory of finished goods	12,000	
Add Finished goods purchased	488,000	
	500,000	
Deduct Closing inventory of finished goods	30,000	
Cost of finished inventory sold		470,000
Gross profit		490,000
Less Expenses:		
Wages and salaries	150,000	
Selling and distribution	75,000	
Heating and lighting	45,000	
Depreciation	70,000	
Financing charges	35,000	
Miscellaneous	15,000	
		390,000
Net profit		100,000

Balance sheet of Trader Co. as at 31 August

	£	£		£	£
Fixed assets			Capital		
Land and buildings		4,050,000	Reserves:		4,600,000
Plant and machinery	3,864,000		Retained profit		875,000
Less depreciation	1,800,000		Loan		1,725,000
		2,064,000			
Fixtures and fittings	1,266,000				
Less depreciation	200,000				
		1,066,000			
Motor vehicles	65,000				
Less depreciation	45,000				
		20,000			
Current assets:			Current liabilities:		
Inventory	30,000		Creditors	40,000	
Debtors	20,000		Accruals	10,000	
Bank	—				50,000
		50,000			
		7,250,000			7,250,000

PROFITABILITY RATIOS

These control ratios are concerned with the return on the long-term investment in the organisation, that is, the return on the capital employed – and with the return on the sales. They show how much the sales contribute to fixed costs (the costs do not change with the level of activity, like salaries) and whether there is enough left over for a profit.

We will look first at the return on the capital employed. The most accepted measure of capital employed is the 'net capital employed', which is the total assets minus the current liabilities.

Gross profit as a percentage of the net capital employed

This is calculated using the formula:

$$\frac{\text{Gross profit} \times 100}{\text{Net capital employed}}$$

Using our example, this calculation becomes:

$$\frac{\text{£}490,000 \times 100}{(\text{£}7,250,000 - \text{£}50,000)} = \frac{\text{£}49,000,000}{\text{£}7,200,000} = 6.8\%$$

This figure in isolation is of little or no value, but if a trend over five years is obtained we can see whether management is able to exercise control over the organisation's operations. In this example the gross profit is largely dependent on the difference between the buying-price and the selling-price, and once a figure has been accepted as reasonable for the gross profit as a percentage of the net capital employed it should not alter significantly unless the management decides that it should. If a return of 6.7 per cent is considered acceptable, and over five years the actual results have been 6.6 per cent, 6.7 per cent, 6.7 per cent and 6.8 per cent, then analysts would be happy that, at least with regard to the buying and selling of goods, the organisation was operating satisfactorily. On the other hand, a set of results showing 6.0 per cent, 7.2 per cent, 5.8 per cent, 6.3 per cent and 7.0 per cent would leave a serious question-mark over the management of the undertaking.

Whenever performance is being measured it should be remembered that one figure in isolation is useless. Only a set of results showing a trend over five years or so can be meaningful, and the average for the industry or business sector – which can be found in publications like 'Dun and Bradstreet' – may also be helpful.

Net profit as a percentage of the net capital employed (often referred to as the primary ratio)
This is calculated using the formula:

$$\frac{\text{Net profit} \times 100}{\text{Net capital employed}}$$

Using our example, this calculation becomes:

$$\frac{£100,000 \times 100}{£7,250,000 - £50,000} = \frac{£10,000,000}{£7,200,000} = 1.4\%$$

This figure shows the overall return on the long-term investment in the business and can be compared with the return that could be earned from investing the money safely in a bank, building society or in national savings. Clearly 1.4 per cent is far less than could be earned almost anywhere else with the money. Using this criterion, the result for the year is poor. To discover whether it is a freak result we need the average for the last five years as well as the average for the business sector in which the concern operates. If it is a true representation of the return the organisation makes, then in purely financial terms the company should be closed down and the money invested where it would earn a higher return. There may, however, be good reasons for remaining in business: perhaps it is providing a valuable service, or the owners may enjoy what they are doing so much that they do not wish to close.

It is always dangerous to make decisions on limited information, but ratios do highlight areas that require investigation.

Gross profit as a percentage of sales

This is calculated using the formula:

$$\frac{\text{Gross profit} \times 100}{\text{Sales}}$$

Using our example, this calculation becomes:

$$\frac{£490,000 \times 100}{£960,000} = \frac{£49,000,000}{£960,000} = 51\%$$

This figure is a useful control ratio, in that it represents the difference between the buying-price and the selling-price of the goods and, once it has been decided upon, should not alter from period to period. Again it is of little use in isolation, but a trend over five or more years will reveal much about the way in which the undertaking is being controlled. The gross profit as a percentage of sales is a reflection of the 'mark-up', the amount that has been added to the cost price of the goods to arrive at the selling-price. The calculation of the mark-up is (selling-price − cost price) as a percentage of the cost price, which in this example is:

$$\frac{(£960,000 - £470,000) \times 100}{£470,000} = \frac{£490,000 \times 100}{£470,000}$$

$$= \frac{£49,000,000}{£470,000} = 104.3\%$$

This is to say that the concern is adding 104.3 per cent to the cost price of the goods to arrive at the selling-price. This may sound a lot, but it should be remembered that all the running costs of the organisation as well as the profit have to be met out of this figure.

Net profit as a percentage of sales

This is calculated using the formula:

$$\frac{\text{Net profit} \times 100}{\text{Sales}}$$

Using our example, this calculation becomes:

$$\frac{\pounds 100,000 \times 100}{\pounds 960,000} = \frac{\pounds 10,000,000}{\pounds 960,000} = 10.4\%$$

This represents the percentage of sales that is left over for profit once all the other expenses have been met. When compared with the average for the industry and a trend over five or more years, it is possible to see whether the undertaking is performing better or worse than average, and whether it is improving or deteriorating with time. In common with all ratios, this one does not provide a definitive answer but indicates where it may be necessary to investigate further. Even activities like recruitment and training are inextricably linked with profitability ratios (hence the need for the personnel manager to understand them and always keep in mind the position of the business). After all, when an organisation is failing to make good use of its resources there is little point in recruiting additional people who may shortly have to be released; and staff who require training often need help in defining their needs, and may then be gently oriented towards the likely future direction of the whole business.

LIQUIDITY RATIOS

These are concerned with an undertaking's ability to pay its way in the medium- and short-term future. Like all other ratios, they do not indicate much about the organisation when taken on their own, but used in conjunction with the average for the sector and the trend over the last five or more years they become good indicators of overall liquidity.

Current ratio

This is given by current assets as a ratio of current liabilities, with the current liabilities represented as unity (1). In our example we have current assets of £50,000 and current liabilities of £50,000. To express this as a ratio, we have current assets : current liabilities, and this becomes £50,000 : £50,000. Because the current liabilities are always shown as 1, to arrive at the figure for the current assets we divide the current assets by the current liabilities:

$$\frac{\text{Current assets}}{\text{Current liabilities}} = \frac{\text{£50,000}}{\text{£50,000}} = 1$$

So we have the current ratio of 1 : 1.

This indicates the firm's ability to pay its way in the medium term – that is, for about four to nine months into the future. We can see that the current assets just cover the current liabilities but have no indication as to whether that is good or bad. Some organisations, like Williams Holdings in the manufacturing sector, for example, have a current ratio of 1.4 : 1, whereas Tesco Stores has a current ratio of 0.37 : 1, so it is important to know the average for the sector and the trend for this ratio, where changes may be far more important than the actual figure.

Quick ratio (acid test)

This is given by the quick assets as a ratio of the current liabilities. The 'quick' assets are those that can be readily turned into cash. These obviously exclude fixed assets and normally also exclude the figure for inventory. In our example we have quick assets of £20,000 and current liabilities of £50,000, giving a quick ratio or acid test of:

$$20,000 : 50,000 = \frac{\text{£20,000}}{\text{£50,000}} = 0.4$$

A ratio of 0.4 : 1 like this seems extremely low, but when compared with a company such as Tesco, which runs on a low quick ratio of 0.09 : 1, it appears less of a problem.

Looking at the balance sheet, we see that there is no money and that there are relatively low debtors of £20,000 against creditors of £40,000. Much depends on how quickly inventory can be turned into money, and it would be interesting to see the trend over the last five or more years, but alarm signals are certainly flashing and further investigation is required into the short-term liquidity of the Trader Co.

The long-term solvency ratios, gearing and interest cover

The long-term solvency ratio – often referred to in the UK as the 'gearing ratio' and in America as the 'leverage' – is of great importance to personnel managers and others. The higher the gearing – that is to say, the greater the borrowing as a proportion of the total long-term financing – the higher the risk of business failure. This is due to the fact that money is a valuable asset that has to be paid for through interest – the more the borrowing, the greater the amount of money that has to be found. This can lead to cash-flow problems when profits fall, and even possible business failure. Management should borrow enough to benefit the business but not so much as to cause problems. It is here that the gearing ratio can be helpful. If your organisation's gearing ratio is below the average for the business sector, no major problems should ensue. On the other hand, if it goes above the average, alarms should sound and pertinent questions should be asked.

Interest cover is another long-term solvency ratio that is becoming more popular than the gearing ratio. It is calculated by dividing the profit before interest by the interest charged. Trends are important, but if the ratio falls below 1.5 times, questions should be asked.

EFFICIENCY RATIOS OR ACTIVITY RATIOS

Efficiency ratios indicate how effectively the inventory, creditors and debtors of the concern are being managed. These latter all form part of the working capital, which, remember, is current assets minus current liabilities. Lack of working capital means that the organisation cannot be run effectively, so it has to be carefully managed. There are three major efficiency ratios.

Rate of inventory turnover, or age of inventory

This tells the organisation how many times the inventory is changed in a year, or how long on average it is held before being used. The objective of most organisations is to hold as little inventory as possible for as short a time as possible. The advent of the 'just-in-time' system of inventory management is an attempt to hold no inventory at all but to buy stock as it is needed. This is proving extremely difficult to achieve in practice, but there is certainly a strong move towards it. Money tied up in inventory is regarded by many as dead money that could be put to better use elsewhere.

In calculating the speed with which inventory is being used we employ the formula: cost of inventory used divided by the year-end inventory or, where there is sufficient information, by the average inventory holding during the period under review. A rough average inventory holding is given by:

$$\frac{\text{Opening inventory} + \text{Closing inventory}}{2}$$

Trader Co. has opening inventory of £12,000 and closing inventory of £30,000, which gives an average inventory of:

$$\frac{£12,000 + £30,000}{2} = \frac{£42,000}{2} = £21,000$$

The cost of inventory used is the cost of finished inventory sold, £470,000, and the number of times the inventory has been turned over is given by dividing £470,000 by £21,000: 22.4 times a year. It is therefore held on average for:

$$\frac{52}{22.4} \quad \text{or 2.32 weeks}$$

This would be regarded as quite fast for most concerns, but a petrol retailer or fast-food shop would be very unhappy with it, so again we need to look at the average for the sector and the trend over the last five or more years before we can begin to draw any conclusions.

Speed of turnover of creditors, or age of creditors

This indicates how many times the creditors are turned over (not physically!) in the year, or how many weeks they are kept waiting for their money. Most managers try to ensure that they are not paying their suppliers any more quickly than they receive money from their customers.

In calculating the speed with which we pay our suppliers we apply the formula: credit purchases (if the credit purchases are not known the total purchases figure is used) divided by the year-end creditors. Using the figures in our example, we have £488,000 divided by £40,000: 12 per year. This shows that on average they have had to wait 52/12 = 4.3 weeks for their money. This is very quick by today's standards. Most organisations keep their suppliers waiting more than 4.3 weeks, but once again the figure should be treated with care and should be compared with the trend over five or more years, the industry average and the speed with which money is collected from customers.

Speed of turnover of debtors, or age of debtors

This indicates the number of times the debtors are turned over in the year, or how many weeks they take to pay for the goods they have received from the concern. The formula used is: credit sales (if known, otherwise the total sales figure is used) divided by the year-end debtors. Using the figures in our example, we have £960,000 divided by £20,000. This means we have collected money from our customers approximately 48 times in 52 weeks, showing that on average the organisation has had to wait approximately one week for its money. (Using the alternative convention of working in days and assuming 360 working days in a year, 360/48 = 7.5 days, which again indicates that virtually all the sales are converted into cash in one week).

We can now investigate the quick ratio or acid test further in the light of this new information. The acid test was 0.4 : 1, which appeared to indicate short-term liquidity problems, but we now know that sales are converted into cash within a week, and suppliers are kept waiting four weeks for their money. Assuming sales take place evenly throughout the year, the daily value of goods sold is:

$$\frac{£960,000}{360} = £2,667$$

In other words, the creditors of £40,000 could be paid from 15 days' sales, so what at first sight appears to be a serious liquidity problem turns out to be more manageable when additional information is available.

The liquidity and efficiency ratios are key indicators that enable management to ensure that the organisation will survive and is successfully meeting the operating targets. Because the personnel manager is often an important member of the executive team, present at meetings where critical decisions are made, a good knowledge of the financial ratios is essential if he or she is to contribute fully to the discussion.

Exercise 11

Apply these ratios where possible to Exercises 7–10 at the end of Chapter 5, and state whether you feel things are improving or deteriorating. Then compare your answers with the sample ones given at the end of the book.

WORKING THROUGH A PRACTICAL EXAMPLE: SAINSBURY'S

We have considered the ratios of fictitious organisations and seen how they are calculated. It is important for personnel managers to understand them and their purpose so that they can use them to reinforce any points that they may wish to make either in discussions with individuals or in meetings. Let us now apply what we have learned to the accounts of a highly respected organisation: Sainsbury's.

Group profit and loss account

for the 52 weeks to 7 March 1998

	1998 £m	1997 £m
Group sales including VAT and sales taxes	15,496	14,312
VAT and sales taxes	996	917
Group sales excluding VAT and sales taxes	14,500	13,395
Cost of sales	13,289	12,363
Exceptional cost of sales – Texas Homecare integration costs	–	50
Gross profit	1,211	982
Administrative expenses	357	287
Year 2000 costs	20	–
Group operating profit before profit-sharing	834	695
Profit-sharing	44	37
Group operating profit	790	658
Associated Undertakings – share of profit	16	19
Profit on sale of properties	3	8
Loss on disposal of a subsidiary	(12)	–
Profit on ordinary activities before interest	797	685
Net interest payable	78	76
Profit on ordinary activities before tax	719	609
Tax on profit on ordinary activities	236	208
Profit on ordinary activities after tax	483	401
Minority equity interest	4	2
Profit for the financial year	487	403
Equity dividends	264	226
Retained profit	223	177
Earnings per share	26.1p	22.0
Exceptional cost of sales	–	1.8
Loss/(profit) on sale of properties and disposal of a subsidiary	0.5p	(0.4)
Earnings per share before exceptional cost of sales and loss/profit on sale of properties and disposal of a subsidiary	26.6p	23.4
Fully diluted earnings per share	25.7p	21.8
Fully diluted earnings per share before exceptional cost of sales and loss/profit on sale of properties and disposal of a subsidiary	26.2p	23.1

Group balance sheet
7 March 1998

	1998 £m	1997 £m
Fixed assets		
Tangible assets	6,133	5,893
Investments	151	148
	6,284	6,041
Current assets		
Stocks	743	744
Debtors	229	236
Investments	14	7
Sainsbury's Bank	1,548	17
Cash and liquid funds	270	241
	2,804	1,245
Creditors: due within one year		
Sainsbury's Bank	(1,502)	(7)
Other	(2,499)	(2,797)
	(4,001)	(2,804)
Net current liabilities	(1,197)	(1,559)
Total assets less current liabilities	5,087	4,482
Creditors: due after one year		
Convertible Capital Bonds	–	(156)
Other	(949)	(595)
Provisions for liabilities and charges	(24)	(55)
Total net assets	4,114	3,676
Capital and reserves		
Called-up share capital	476	460
Share premium account	1,295	1,097
Revaluation reserve	38	33
Profit and loss account	2,303	2,081
Equity shareholders' funds	4,112	3,671
Minority equity interest	38	5
Total capital employed	4,150	3,676

The Summary Financial Statement was approved by the Board of Directors on 5 May 1998, and is signed on its behalf by

Lord Sainsbury of Turville *Chairman*

Ten-year financial record

	1989	1990	1991	1992	1993	1994††	1995	1996†††	1997††††	1998†††††
Results (£ million)										
Group sales (including VAT and sales taxes)	5,915	7,257	8,201	9,202	10,270	11,224	12,065	13,499	14,312	15,496
Increase on previous year	18.1%	22.7%	13.0%	12.2%	11.6%	9.3%	7.5%	11.9%	6.0%	8.3%
Group operating profit (before Year 2000 costs and profit sharing)										
Sainsbury's Supermarkets	342	409	516	604	716	697	784	744	662	735
Savacentre	–	17	23	28	36	38	41	34	30	31
Homebase	9	11	13	15	18	23	31	26	16	55
Shaw's	22	34	30	21	19	31	40	51	41	38
Sainsbury's Bank	–	–	–	–	–	–	–	–	(6)	(15)
Other operating activities	–	–	3	(2)	(4)	7	3	(1)	2	10
	373	471	585	666	785	796	899	854	745	854
Year 2000 costs	–	–	–	–	–	–	–	–	–	(20)
Profit-sharing	(27)	(34)	(44)	(49)	(59)	(56)	(61)	(50)	(37)	(44)
Associates	16	1	–	1	–	–	6	19	19	16
Interest receivable/(payable)	(10)	(18)	(36)	13	9	(9)	(36)	(59)	(76)	(78)
Group profit before tax and property items	352	420	505	631	735	731	808	764	651	728
Increase/(decrease) on previous year	18.1%	19.3%	20.2%	25.0%	16.5%	(0.5)%	10.5%	(5.4)%	(14.8)%	11.8%
Profit/(loss) on sale of fixed assets	23	31	13	(3)	(2)	7	1	(4)	8	3
Group profit before tax	375	451	518	628	733	738	809	760	659	731
Increase/(decrease) on previous year	21.8%	20.3%	14.9%	21.2%	16.7%	0.7%	9.6%	(6.1)%	(13.3)%	10.9%
Earnings per share★										
Basic	16.57p	20.57p	23.11p	25.69p	28.47p	28.0p	29.8p	26.8p	22.0p	26.1p
Increase/(decrease) on previous year	23.5%	24.1%	12.4%	11.2%	10.8%	(1.6)%	6.3%	(10.1)%	(17.9)%	18.6%
Fully diluted (before exceptional costs and excluding profit/loss on sale of fixed assets)	14.44p	18.15p	21.74p	25.34p	28.07p	27.0p	29.0p	27.8p	23.1p	26.2p
Increase/(decrease) on previous year	11.9%	25.7%	19.7%	16.6%	10.8%	(3.7)%	7.4%	(4.1)%	(16.9)%	13.4%
Dividend per share★	4.99p	6.03p	7.27p	8.75p	10.0p	10.6p	11.7p	12.1p	12.3p	13.9p

★ Adjusted in respect of capitalisation issues in 1984 and 1987 and rights issue in 1991.
† Property profits for 1992 restated to comply with FRS 3.
†† 1994 figures for profits and earnings per share are stated before exceptional costs of £369.5 million but after changes in accounting for depreciation of £38.7 million.
††† 1996 figures for profits and fully diluted earnings per share are stated before exceptional costs of £48 million.
†††† 1997 figures for profits and fully diluted earnings per share are stated before exceptional costs of £50 million.
††††† 1998 figures for profits and fully diluted earnings per share are stated before a loss of £12 million on the disposal of a subsidiary.

	1989	1990	1991	1992	1993	1994	1995	1996	1997	1998
Retail statistics										
Number of outlets at										
financial year-end										
Sainsbury's Supermarkets –										
over 40,000 sq ft sales										
area	7	7	8	12	12	12	14	16	21	26
25,000 – 40,000 sq ft										
sales area	88	109	128	147	165	181	194	211	223	229
15,000 – 25,000 sq ft										
sales area	110	106	102	98	99	99	98	87	87	93
under 15,000 sq ft sales										
area	87	69	61	56	52	49	49	49	47	43
Sainsbury's Supermarkets	292	291	299	313	328	341	355	363	378	391
Savacentre	7	8	9	9	9	10	10	12	12	13
Homebase	48	55	61	64	70	76	83	310	297	298
Shaw's	61	66	70	73	79	87	87	96	115	121
Total number of stores	**408**	**420**	**439**	**459**	**486**	**514**	**535**	**781**	**802**	**823**
Sales area (000 sq ft)										
Sainsbury's Supermarkets	5,964	6,434	6,951	7,632	8,303	8,827	9,338	9,767	10,387	10,860
Savacentre	543	665	798	798	798	864	864	1,034	1,034	1,119
Homebase (approx.										
80% covered sales area)	1,886	2,107	2,317	2,406	2,609	2,810	3,082	11,632	11,246▲	11,201
Shaw's	1,693	1,928	2,107	2,229	2,448	2,740	2,762	3,137	3,822	4,119
Group total	**10,086**	**11,134**	**12,173**	**13,065**	**14,158**	**15,241**	**16,046**	**25,570**§	**26,489**▲	**27,299**
Net increase on previous										
year:										
Sainsbury's Supermarkets	9.2%	7.9%	8.0%	9.8%	8.8%	6.3%	5.8%	4.6%	6.3%	4.6%
Group	10.45	10.4%	9.3%	7.3%	8.4%	7.6%	5.3%	59.1%	3.6%	3.1%
New Sainsbury's										
Supermarket openings	20	22	20	21	23	23	20	10	18	19
Average Sainsbury's										
Supermarkets sales										
(including VAT)★★										
Per square foot										
(£ per week)	16.50	17.26	18.17	18.51	18.84	18.60	18.53	18.59	18.69	18.87
Share of national trade										
in predominantly food										
stores and pharm-										
aceutical, medical,										
cosmetic and toilet										
goods outlets★★★	10.1%	10.8%	11.3%	11.7%	12.3%	12.4%	12.6%	12.5%	12.6%	12.7%

▲ Restated to exclude concession areas.

★★ Excluding petrol.

★★★ Based on Central Statistical Office/Office for National Statistics (Re-based during 1995) and Sainsbury's Supermarkets and Savacentre sales, excluding petrol.

§ Excluding Texas – Group total = 17,408,000 sq ft. Net increase 1,362,000 sq ft; increase of 8.5 per cent.

Source: J Sainsbury plc *Annual Review 1998*.

1 Profitability Ratios   *1997*   *1998*

A. Gross profit to net capital employed

$$\frac{982 \times 100}{4,482} \quad = \quad 21.9\% \quad 23.6\%$$

$$\frac{\text{Gross profit} \times 100}{\text{Net capital employed}}$$

B. Net profit to net capital employed

$$\frac{\text{Profit on ordinary activities before tax} \times 100}{\text{Net capital employed}}$$

$$\frac{609 \times 100}{4,482} \quad = \quad 13.6\% \quad 14.0\%$$

C. Gross profit percentage of sales

$$\frac{\text{Gross Profit} \times 100}{\text{Sales}} \quad \frac{982 \times 100}{14,312} \quad = \quad 6.9\% \quad 7.8\%$$

D. Net profit percentage of sales

$$\frac{\text{Net Profit} \times 100}{\text{Sales}} \quad \frac{609 \times 100}{14,312} \quad = \quad 4.3\% \quad 4.6\%$$

2 Short-term liquidity ratios

A. Current ratio

Current assets : Current liabilities

$$1245 : 2804 \quad = \quad 0.44 : 1 \quad 0.71 : 1$$

B. Quick ratio

Quick assets : Current liabilities

$$501 : 2,804 \quad = \quad 0.18 : 1 \quad 0.52 : 1$$

3 Long-term solvency ratio

A. Gearing ratio

$$\frac{\text{Borrowing} \times 100}{\text{Equity}}$$

$$= \quad \frac{(156 + 595) \times 100}{3671} = \quad 20.5\% \quad 23.1\%$$

B. Interest cover

$$\frac{\text{Profit before interest}}{\text{Interest}} \quad = \quad \frac{685}{76} \quad = \quad \begin{array}{cc} 9 & 10.2 \\ \text{times} & \text{times} \end{array}$$

4 Efficiency or activity ratios   *1997*   *1998*

A. Collection period for debts (Age of debtors)

$$\frac{\text{Turnover}}{\text{Trade debtors}}$$

$$\frac{14{,}312}{236} = 60.6 \text{ times}$$ 6 days   5.3 days

B. Payment period for creditors (Age of creditors)

$$\frac{\text{Cost of sales}}{\text{Trade creditors}} =$$

$$\frac{12{,}363}{2{,}797} = 4.4 \text{ times}$$ 82 days   67.9 days

C. Rate of stock turnover

$$\frac{\text{Cost of Sales}}{\text{Year-end stock}}$$

$$\frac{12{,}363}{744} = 16.6 \text{ times} =$$ 22.6 days   20.1 days

D. Fixed asset turnover

$$\frac{\text{Turnover (sales)}}{\text{Tangible fixed assets}}$$

$$\frac{14{,}312}{5{,}893} =$$ 2.4 times   2.5 times

E. Number of employees

Sainsbury's Supermarkets	127,000
Savacentre	10,000
Homebase	17,000
Sainsbury's Bank	20,000
	174,000

Sales per employee (1998)

$$\frac{\text{Turnover (sales)}}{\text{Number of employees}} \quad \frac{15{,}496 \text{ million}}{174{,}000} = \quad - \quad £89{,}057$$

Having calculated the ratios, what have they told you about Sainsbury's? What additional information would be helpful in getting a feel for the group's performance?

How would a personnel manager employ the following ratios?

1 Gross profit to net capital employed

2 Net profit percentage sales

3 Interest cover

4 Rate of stock turnover

5 Sales per employee.

Obtain the accounts of your concern and assess its performance over two recent years. Decide whether it is improving, and highlight its strengths and weaknesses.

8 Financial implications of personnel decisions

At the end of this chapter the reader should understand the financial implications of personnel decisions and some of the ways in which they can be calculated. The management competencies that this chapter is intended to develop are those of reviewimg the generation and allocation of financial resources and obtaining financial resources for the organisation's activities.

The main decisions of the personnel manager concern human resources – but there are other decisions that are important, such as investing in capital equipment or training services outside the employing organisation. Each of these decisions will generate both costs and revenues, and it is essential that the personnel manager fully appreciates their implications.

People are essential to the success of all organisations. They are the major asset of any undertaking, but they are also a major cost. It is because of this that it is important to ensure that organisations are using their people effectively, efficiently and economically. In the private sector a key ratio that is successfully utilised is sales per employee (see the analysis of Sainsbury's accounts in Chapter 7). Do you know what the equivalent figure is in your business? You should be aware that if you recruit additional people it will have an immediate impact on the sales-per-employee ratio. This ratio, like the others we have considered, should never be considered in isolation. Trends are significant, as are comparisons with other similar businesses. Using the manufacturing account example in Chapter 6 (Example 16, page 57) and assuming that there are 5,000 employees, we can calculate the sales per employee to be:

$$\frac{\text{Sales}}{\text{Employees}} \quad \frac{7{,}600{,}000}{5{,}000} \quad = \quad \pounds 1{,}520$$

If you were presented with this figure in isolation, your reaction would probably be 'So what!' In order to be meaningful it has to be compared with something. If sales per employee had been £2,000 for the last four years and it suddenly fell to £1,520, you would want to know why, and to correct the situation if possible. Recruitment of additional staff would have an impact on the ratio unless you were immediately able to generate proportionately higher sales. For example, an extra 100 staff would make the sales per employee:

$$\frac{£7,600,000}{5,100} \quad = \quad £1,490.20$$

This fall of nearly £30 per employee would have to be recovered as quickly as possible. Sales are not as critical in the public sector as they are in the private sector, so the above ratio would not apply. But it might be replaced by such ratios as refuse collected per employee, houses painted per employee or meals served per employee.

This concentration on the activity per employee has led many organisations, and managers within them, to believe that the way to save money and operate more effectively is by reducing the number of staff. There is a great emphasis on headcount and the personnel manager has to demonstrate the added value provided by staff, particularly his or her own department. It is incumbent on the personnel manager to provide information that demonstrates the efficiency of the department, and if this can be achieved through the use of ratios, so much the better. One ratio commonly used for this purpose is the cost of human resources, which is calculated by dividing the expenses of each department by the total expenses of the organisation. If the expenses of an organisation are £6,740,000, and of the personnel, manufacturing, sales and marketing departments are £960,000, £3,400,000, £1,230,000 and £1,150,000 respectively, then the ratio for each department becomes:

$$\text{Personnel} \quad \frac{£960,000}{£6,740,000} \quad \times \ 100 \quad = \quad 14.2\%$$

Manufacturing $\dfrac{£3,400,000}{£6,740,000}$ $\times$ 100 = 50.45%

Sales $\dfrac{£1,230,000}{£6,740,000}$ $\times$ 100 = 18.25%

Marketing $\dfrac{£1,150,000}{£6,740,000}$ $\times$ 100 = 17.1%

This could then be illustrated as follows:

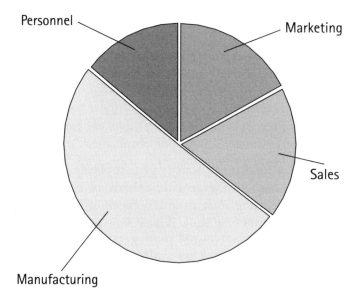

To be able to undertake such an investigation the personnel manager would require more information than is provided by the traditional financial accounts, and it is for reasons like this that the cost accounts – to which we will be introduced in the next chapter – were developed.

The capital investment decision has a major impact on the organisation. By its nature it uses a large proportion of the available money and may carry over for more than one financial year. If, for example, the personnel manager requires a new training wing costing £4 million, it is extremely unlikely that the proposal will be accepted unless the budgeted benefits can be seen to exceed the costs by a satisfactory amount. It is no use talking in general terms about the benefits that will accrue to the organisation from such a step. Estimates have to be made of the savings and/or income that will be generated by the scheme, and they must be compared with the outlay. The personnel manager will then be able to build a case for the proposal and hopefully demonstrate its advantages over competing bids for the available funds for capital outlay. He or she can employ such tools as pay-back, which demonstrates how quickly the expenditure is recovered, and net present value, which compares the outlay with the estimate of funds to be generated in present-value terms. These approaches are discussed in greater detail in Chapter 16.

Many organisations are now offering to the open market expertise that they previously employed internally. Training is one such service, and it is reasonable that this should be so. Undertakings that have been proactive in training and development over the last six years have found that other organisations are prepared to pay well for their expertise. But the personnel manager should not embark on such a course of action without fully considering the attendant costs and benefits. There is more than one way of calculating the costs of such a venture. If the full-cost approach is adopted, all costs would have to be recovered plus the required profit. This approach is fully discussed in Chapter 10. On the other hand, the concept of contribution may be applied, using the marginal costing approach. Here only those costs directly involved in providing the additional training are considered; any income over and above that makes a contribution to the departmental fixed costs. Chapter 12 covers this approach in greater detail.

Why are people important to organisations?

What is the cost of human resources ratio?

Why are undertakings offering training on the open market?

Ascertain the financial information that the personnel manager in your organisation considers to be the most important to enable him or her to make better decisions.

9 Costing and human resources

At the end of this chapter the reader should understand how cost accounts are prepared, their link with the financial accounts, and the human resource implication. The management competence that the chapter is intended to develop is that of reviewing the generation and allocation of financial resources and controlling expenditure against budget.

The information systems that have been dealt with so far have been concerned with financial information for planning and reporting, with some control elements. In Chapter 6 manufacturing accounts were discussed, and it was suggested that these lend themselves to calculating the cost per unit produced. Because information of this nature is the basis for exercising control in an organisation, it will be investigated more fully.

The accounts that we have examined up till now are the financial accounts which give an overview of the position of an organisation. Although this information can help the personnel manager (and other managers) to control the finances for which he or she is responsible and to make bids for resources, more detailed information is required if costs are to be controlled and plans monitored. This is provided by the cost accounts, which must be capable of being reconciled with the financial accounts at all times. Costing is the process of analysing the expenditure of an organisation into the separate costs for each of the services or products supplied to customers, and includes training.

The way in which the cost and financial accounts may be reconciled is shown in the following simple example.

Example 18

Financial Accounts
(in thousands of pounds)

Earnings	1,432
Expenses	1,141
Profit	291

Cost Accounts
(in thousands of pounds)

Service	Cleaning	Security	Training	Transport	TOTAL
Earnings	680	415	123	214	1,432
Expenses	630	372	9	130	1,141
Profit	50	43	114	84	291

Without the benefit of the cost accounts, the planning team might have been inclined to concentrate on cleaning, which generates the largest earnings. An examination of the cost accounts, however, clearly shows that training gives the greatest profit and would possibly be an appropriate area to develop. Cost accounts, then, can assist a personnel manager in making a case for the contribution made by the personnel department to the health of the organisation as a whole. But, as we have seen, it is essential for the cost accounts to be reconciled with the financial accounts. If they are not, they are no value to managers and their preparation is a waste of time.

The purposes of costing can be stated to be to:

• enable work in progress and finished goods to be valued for short-term and annual accounts

• provide the basis for tenders, pricing policies and estimates

• maintain control over the costs of an organisation

• provide information to ensure that decisions are made on the correct basis.

The costs of each department consist of three elements:

• labour

- materials

- overheads.

These three elements of cost are further broken down into *direct costs*, which are charged directly to the service or product, and *indirect costs*, which are apportioned to the service or product on some equitable basis, as outlined in Chapter 10. The cost accounts and the financial accounts are combined in the following way:

	Direct labour
+	Direct materials
+	Direct expense (ie any other expenses directly attributable to the product produced, ————————— such as electricity)
=	PRIME COST
+	Factory overhead
=	PRODUCTION COST
+	Selling and distribution overhead
+	Selling and distribution direct expense
+	Administration overhead
=	COST OF SALES taken from EARNINGS
=	NET PROFIT

The manager also needs to know whether the costs with which he or she is dealing are fixed – whether they remain constant for any level of activity within prescribed limits – or whether they are variable – whether they vary directly with changes in the level of activity. An example of a fixed cost might be staff salaries in a department which employed three trainers, each capable of training between 10 and 20 people. Their combined salaries would be £51,000 whether they were training 30 people or 60 people a week. However, if they were asked to train 100 people a week, the departmental salary bill would become £68,000 because an additional trainer would have to be employed. The fixed-cost line on a graph would then appear as in Figure 7.

Figure 7 Fixed costs in a training department

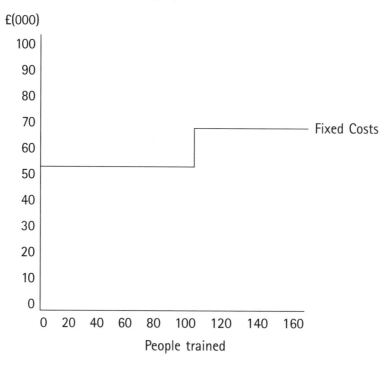

A variable cost would be the cost of the information pack and other materials given to each trainee on the programme. Taking the cost per trainee as £50, the variable cost line could be illustrated as in Figure 8.

You can see from this that if there were no trainees the cost would be zero, whereas for 100 the cost is £5,000. This is helpful to a personnel manager who is costing the service provided against the revenues generated by it.

The next three chapters describe various costing methods and their application by the personnel manager. They also contain examples of the ways in which costs can be calculated and used. It is essential for the personnel manager to fully understand and control the costs that relate to the human resource department.

Figure 8 Variable costs in a training department

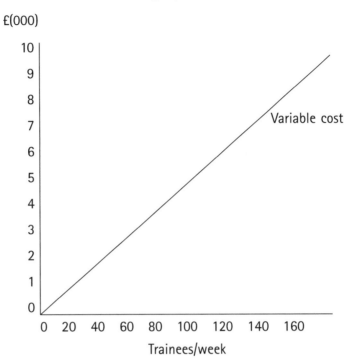

£(000)

What is a direct cost?

What is a fixed cost?

Why do cost accounts and financial accounts have to be reconciled?

What is the prime cost a total of?

Ascertain the fixed and variable costs that relate to your department.

10 Absorption costing

At the end of this chapter the reader should understand how fixed costs are apportioned to the personnel department, why the apportionment often gives rise to concern, and how absorption costing and activity-based costing differ. The management competences that this chapter is intended to develop are those of reviewing the generation and allocation of financial resources.

Standard costing is useful in enabling managers to calculate the expected cost of a unit of production or service. Absorption costing, or total costing as it is sometimes called, helps to ensure that organisational costs are fully recovered when a price is quoted for a job or a unit of consultancy. Because little can be done to alter fixed costs in the short term, they are often overlooked when prices are being calculated, with disastrous results for the organisation. We have seen that one example of a fixed cost is salaries. Others are financing charges, rents, business rates, heating, and depreciation.

Variable costs include the materials used in making a product or providing a service. They also include any labour cost that is charged at an hourly rate for that job or service. These variable costs are relatively easy to control because they can be readily identified and action can be taken to correct the situation if they are seen to be moving in an unexpected way.

Semi-variable costs behave as though they are a combination of fixed and variable costs, with an element that is fixed and an element that alters with the level of activity. An example of such a cost would be maintenance, which has a planned fixed element whatever the level of activity and a variable element that alters with activity. Such costs are extremely difficult to identify.

Example 19
We can now study an example that illustrates the use of absorption costing through the medium of a manufacturing organisation which has two departments and a single product. During manufacture the product spends some time in each of the departments. The expected costs for a month are:

	£
Business rates	300
Heating and lighting	60
Depreciation	100
Salaries	6,000
Administration	400

The resources allocated to the two departments are:

Department	A	B
Floor area (square metres)	20	40
Number of employees	5	15
Value of machinery (in thousands)	£40	£10
Production labour hours	600	1,800

In order to calculate the amount that must be charged out by the departments for work done, the appropriate overhead cost has to be established. This is calculated first of all by apportioning the overhead costs to the departments on an equitable basis:

Cost	Department		Total	Basis of apportionment
	A	B		
	£	£	£	
Rates	100	200	300	Floor area
Heating and lighting	15	45	60	Number of employees
Depreciation	80	20	100	Value of machinery
Salaries	1,500	4,500	6,000	Labour hours
Administration	100	300	400	Number of employees
Total	1,795	5,065	6,860	

The total overhead allocated to the departments is: Department A, £1,795, Department B, £5,065. It is now necessary to decide how the overheads are to be recovered. One way of doing it would be to calculate the amount of overhead to be charged for each labour hour of work done. To do this it is necessary to divide the overheads allocated to the department by the number of production labour hours expected in the department. Using the example, we have:

	Department	
	A	B
Total overheads allocated (£)	1,795	5,065
Production labour hours	600	1,800
Labour hour rate (£)	2.99	2.81

This is an acceptable approach, but it is by no means the only one. Overheads can be charged at a rate per machine hour or as a percentage of the production wages. However they are charged, this approach will help to ensure that overhead costs are not overlooked when prices are calculated. In order to price a job that is expected to spend two labour hours in Department A and one in Department B, and which would incur material costs of £200 and a wage rate of £6 per hour, it is necessary to carry out the following calculation:

		£
Materials		200
Labour:	A 2 × £6	12
	B 1 × £6	6
Prime or direct cost		218

Add the fixed/overhead cost:

Department A: 2 × £2.99	5.98
Department B: 1 × £2.81	2.81
	226.79

£226.79 is simply the cost of the job. Any profit that was required would have to be added to it. The basis on which the overheads have been allocated, with the reasons for the choice, are:

Chartered Institute of Personnel and Development

Customer Satisfaction Survey

*We would be grateful if you could spend a few minutes answering these questions and return the postcard to CIPD. <u>Please use a black pen to answer</u>. **If you would like to receive a free CIPD pen, please include your name and address.*** IPD MEMBER Y/N

....

1. Title of book ....

2. Date of purchase: month .... year ....

3. How did you acquire this book?
☐ Bookshop ☐ Mail order ☐ Exhibition ☐ Gift ☐ Bought from Author

4. If ordered by mail, how long did it take to arrive:
☐ 1 week ☐ 2 weeks ☐ more than 2 weeks

5. Name of shop .... Town.. Country ....

6. Please grade the following according to their influence on your purchasing decision with 1 as least influential: (please tick)

	1	2	3	4	5
Title					
Publisher					
Author					
Price					
Subject					
Cover					

7. On a scale of 1 to 5 (with 1 as poor & 5 as excellent) please give your impressions of the book in terms of: (please tick)

	1	2	3	4	5
Cover design					
Paper/print quality					
Good value for money					
General level of service					

8. Did you find the book:
Covers the subject in sufficient depth ☐ Yes ☐ No
Useful for your work ☐ Yes ☐ No

9. Are you using this book to help:
☐ In your work ☐ Personal study ☐ Both ☐ Other (please state)

Please complete if you are using this as part of a course

10. Name of academic institution...

11. Name of course you are following? ....

12. Did you find this book relevant to the syllabus? ☐ Yes ☐ No ☐ Don't know

Thank you!

To receive regular information about CIPD books and resources call 020 8263 3387.

Any data or information provided to the CIPD for the purposes of membership and other Institute activities will be processed by means of a computer database or otherwise. You may, from time to time, receive business information relevant to your work from the Institute and its other activities. If you do not wish to receive such information please write to the CIPD, giving your full name, address and postcode. The Institute does not make its membership lists available to any outside organisation.

1795/05/00

2 1

Publishing Department

Chartered Institute of Personnel and Development

CIPD House

Camp Road

Wimbledon

London

SW19 4BR

Rates
Based on floor area, because this is the usual method of charging rates. Department B has twice the floor area of Department A, so the rates are allocated on a basis of two to one – ie two-thirds of £300 = £200 to Department B and one-third of £300 = £100 to Department A.

Heating and lighting
Based on the number of employees, but production labour hours could have been used just as well. Department B has three times as many employees as Department A, so heating and lighting are allocated on the basis of three to one – ie three-quarters of £60 = £45 to Department B and a quarter of £60 = £15 to Department A.

Depreciation
Based on the value of machinery. Department A's machinery is four times as valuable as Department B's, so depreciation is allocated on the basis of four to one – ie four-fifths of £100 = £80 goes to Department A and one-fifth of £100 = £20 to Department B.

Salaries
Based on the number of labour hours, but the number of employees could have just as easily been used. Department B's production labour hours are three times those of Department A, so salaries are allocated on the basis of three to one – ie three-quarters of £6,000 = £4,500 goes to Department B and one-quarter of £6,000 = £1,500 to Department A.

Administration
See if you can calculate this one for yourself and check with the answer given at the end of the book.

We have already seen that organisations usually have large indirect or overhead costs that are not charged directly to the service or product that is being provided. It is necessary to recover all of these costs if an undertaking is to be seen to be running efficiently or making a profit. Any organisation that employs only the direct costs in arriving at the cost of a service or product will soon cease to exist or else become a drain on the resources of the community.

If, for example, a service organisation provided a simple service and consisted of three departments, it would be possible for it to charge what it considered to be a good rate to its customers and find at the end of the year that it was making a loss. This is illustrated in Example 20.

Example 20
Good Service Ltd has three departments and its expected costs and activity for the next year are:

Personnel department: annual fixed costs	£120,000
Finance department: annual fixed costs	£100,000
Service department: annual fixed costs	£90,000
Service department: variable costs:	£40 per hour
Hours of service to be sold during the year:	5,000
Charge to customers per hour:	£100

Ignoring the fixed costs of the personnel and finance departments, a charge of £100 per hour seems to be adequate to give a reasonable profit.

Income 5,000 hours at £100 per hour		£500,000
Expenses:		
Fixed costs of service department	£90,000	
Variable costs 5,000 hours at		
£40 per hour	200,000	
		290,000
Profit		£210,000

It is only when the costs of the other two departments are considered that it becomes apparent that a loss of £10,000 has been incurred. This is calculated as:

	£	£
Surplus from service department		210,000
Less		
Fixed costs of personnel department	120,000	
Fixed costs of finance department	100,000	
		220,000
Loss		10,000

In order to avoid this situation it is necessary to find the total charge per hour to ensure that all costs are recovered, together with any profit the company requires. The way to achieve this is first to calculate the charge per hour to recover the fixed costs. That is the total fixed costs divided by the hours of service you expect to sell.

$$\frac{£120,000 + £100,000 + £90,000}{5,000 \text{ hours}} = \frac{£310,000}{5,000 \text{ hours}} = £62 \text{ per hour}$$

If there is to be any profit, this will require an additional cost per hour to the customers. Good Service Ltd requires £40,000 p.a. profit, which necessitates an additional hourly charge of:

$$\frac{40,000}{5,000} = £8 \text{ per hour}$$

The charge per hour now becomes:	£
Variable cost per hour	£40
Add Fixed costs per hour	62
Add Profit per hour	8
	£110

The 5,000 hours of service earn:

$$5,000 \times £110 = £550,000$$

The costs incurred are:

Fixed costs:		
Service department	£90,000	
Personnel department	120,000	
Finance department	100,000	
		£310,000
Surplus		240,000
Less Variable cost 5,000 hours × £40		200,000
Profit		40,000

In order to explore this a little further let us assume that the total overheads of Poor Real Ltd are £620,000 which are to be allocated to the personnel department, finance department and service department on an equitable basis. There are many ways in which this can be done, including percentage of direct wages, labour hour rate, machine hour rate and number of employees. The number of employees in each of the departments is:

Personnel department	Service department	Finance department
15	12	13

Using this information to apportion the overheads to the three departments we share the £620,000 overheads as follows:

Personnel department $\dfrac{15}{40} \times$ £620,000 = £232,500

Service department $\dfrac{12}{40} \times$ £620,000 = £186,000

Finance department $\dfrac{13}{40} \times$ £620,000 = £201,500

Total as an accuracy check   £620,000

This means that if the organisation is to avoid incurring a loss, the personnel department must earn £232,500, the service department £186,000 and the finance department £201,500; otherwise as is usually the case, the service department must earn enough to ensure that all the organisation's overheads are recovered.

The apportionment of overheads to departments is a major source of organisational controversy. The personnel manager who unexpectedly finds that the department has had £232,500 overheads charged to it is not going to be at all pleased, particularly as these are costs over which he or she has little or no control. The most effective approach is to tackle the person responsible for the allocation of the overheads and ascertain the basis on which it has been done. You may then be able to challenge the allocation and be responsible for a more appropriate figure.

In this chapter we have been considering the traditional absorption methods of allocating overheads, but some people consider that these no longer provide good information for decision-making and control. This concern has encouraged another method of allocating overheads to be developed, called activity-based costing, sometimes referred to as ABC. It is felt to give relevant information to management quickly and so help with decision - making and control. The difference is essentially that activity-based costing apportions overheads according to how much use each support service makes of each activity, whereas absorption costing charges on the basis of some other denominator, eg labour hours. The two methods may be compared diagrammatically in Figures 9 and 10.

Figure 9 Absorption costing

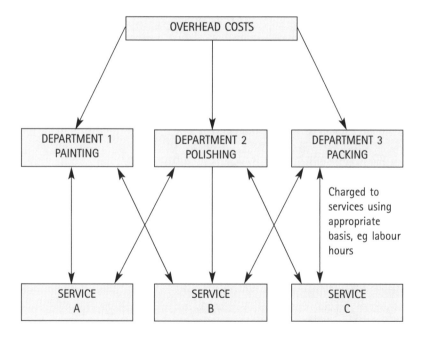

Figure 10 **Activity–based costing**

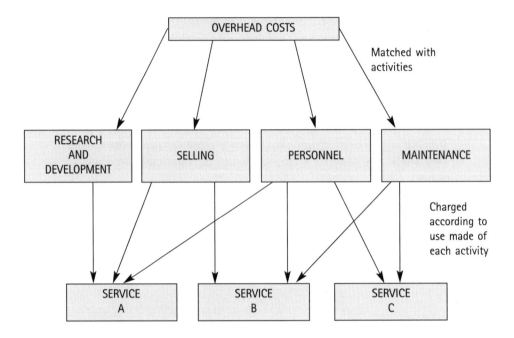

What is absorption costing?

What is activity-based costing?

What is meant by overhead cost apportionment?

On what basis would you expect depreciation to be apportioned?

Does your department have overhead costs apportioned to it? If so, which system is used: absorption costing or activity-based costing?

11 Standard costing

At the end of this chapter the reader should understand the importance of standard costs and the way in which they are set, as well as their use to the personnel manager. The management competence that this chapter is intended to develop is that of controlling expenditure against budgets.

Standard costing is extremely important to personnel managers because it can be used to provide a guide to the expected cost of each training programme offered or of each member of staff recruited. These can then be compared with the actual costs incurred to help ensure that the department is well managed and that costs are properly controlled. Indeed, the system is critical to the efficiency of the organisation as a whole.

The standard cost is the expected cost per unit, and it is derived from a mixture of historical information and forecasting techniques. The more information that is available, the more accurate the standard is likely to be – but it is important to remember that it is a forecast and is therefore rarely, if ever, absolutely correct.

Once the standard has been set, it is crucially important to compare the actual result with the expected result at least monthly, but preferably more often, and, where they differ significantly, ensure that remedial action is taken promptly.

It is here that a good management information system can be extremely helpful. Most organisations are complex, and people in them receive an enormous amount of information, often in the form of computer print-outs. If there are a great number of items that differ from the standard, it will not be possible to correct and report on each one, so two things are necessary.

Firstly, an acceptable difference between the standard and actual results must be decided upon. It will vary from concern to concern but it may be, for example, that anything within ±15 per cent of plan is accepted, whereas anything outside that range has to be reported upon and corrected. Secondly, the system should then ensure that anything outside the ±15 per cent range is highlighted, perhaps by means of an asterisk, so that the person responsible for correcting the situation is made aware of it and takes the necessary action.

SETTING STANDARDS

When a standard costing system is established, the fact that it has tremendous potential for good or ill must be kept in mind. If people feel that it is being foisted upon them without consultation, they will be suspicious and resentful and may cause the system to falter. On the other hand, if they feel that they have been consulted from the beginning and their ideas have been considered, they will feel involved and will want the system to succeed: a sense of ownership is important. In setting the standard or expected cost, too, a great deal of care must be taken. Broadly, there are three approaches that are commonly used.

Perfect standard
This assumes that people in an undertaking can work at peak efficiency throughout the working year. It is, in fact, an impossible target to achieve. If imposed as an actual standard, the effect on morale is devastating: eventually the workforce will become totally demotivated, having gone through a cycle from being well motivated and determined to make the system work to disillusioned failure with no faith in the management of the organisation. Being involved in the discussion, people will work hard to meet the targets, but as they fail to reach them week after week their enthusiasm will wane until the realisation sets in that it is no good trying because the targets cannot be met – and the workforce is totally demoralised.

Slack standard

This assumes that people do not enjoy being faced with a challenge and would rather spend their time talking and doing crosswords than have a demanding job that gives satisfaction through achievement. The target having been set, people will work hard to achieve it, but once they understand that it can be reached week after week with little effort, attention will wander and work will become slipshod. Once again disillusionment will set in as the feeling grows that the organisation neither values its people nor understands their capabilities.

Standard attainable with effort

This assumes that people become well motivated and will do their best if they are involved in decisions and given tasks that stretch them but that can be achieved. In setting the standard, the starting-point is past performance. The standards for previous years are studied, and any scope for improvement within achievable limits is built in to the standard for the next year. Consultation should take place with the staff responsible for achieving the standard, to obtain their support, and this should help to ensure a well-motivated workforce working to good standards of performance. Where possible, those who consistently achieve above-average results should be rewarded in some way, so that people are constantly stimulated to perform well. Realistically, however, it is not always possible to reward good performance in the way that we would like. Much will depend on the culture of the undertaking.

ELEMENTS OF COST

Costs break down into three elements: labour, materials and overheads, which consist of such items as rates, depreciation and the salaries of 'non-productive' workers. Here 'non-productive' means not directly making the goods or providing the service, and standards have to be set for each type of such workers. The detailed control of overhead costs is outside the scope of this book, and the rest of this chapter deals with the control of labour and material costs – the ones that can most readily be changed in the short term.

Labour costs

The expected labour cost of a job or operation can be arrived at by going through the process of reaching an attainable standard (see above). Once it has been set, it is not usually possible to alter a standard very often – in fact it is rarely altered more than once or twice a year. The following illustrations show how labour costs may be controlled, using the labour rate variance and the labour efficiency variance.

Labour rate variance

Caused by changes in rates of pay, and calculated using the formula:

$$\text{Actual hours} \times \text{Change in wage rate per hour}$$

The change in wage rate per hour is the standard or expected wage rate minus the actual wage rate.

Labour efficiency variance

Caused by changes in the speed of production, and calculated using the formula:

$$\text{Standard wage rate per hour} \times \text{Change in the hours worked}$$

The change in the hours worked is the standard hours minus the actual hours.

Example 21

The standard cost is four hours
@ £7 per hour   = £28 per unit.

The actual cost is 380 hours
@ £7.50 per hour   = £2,850 per 100 units

                                      = £28.50 per unit.

The labour rate variance is (380 $\times$ 50p) = £190 adverse

When costs are greater than the standard, the difference

between the budgeted and actual cost is termed an 'adverse' variance. The *variance* is the difference between the expected and the actual cost, and it is adverse because it is more than expected. Had the cost been less than expected, the variance would have been 'favourable'. It must be emphasised that a favourable variance is as bad as an adverse one, since both indicate a failure to work to plan and may need corrective action. The labour rate variance is adverse because the rate has increased from £7 to £7.50 per hour.

The labour efficiency variance is £7 × (400 − 380) = £140 favourable

The variance is favourable because for 100 units you would expect to use 400 hours, but only 380 hours have been used. So the total labour variance is £190 adverse and £140 favourable, which nets down to £50 (£190 − £140) adverse. This can be confirmed by comparing the actual labour cost of £2,850 with the expected labour cost of £2,800 (400 hours at £7 per hour), which confirms the total labour variance of £50 adverse. It therefore shows the calculations of the individual labour variances to be correct.

Material costs
The process described above for setting an attainable standard, when applied to materials, will give the expected material cost of a job or operation, which enables material costs to be controlled through the medium of the material price and material usage variances illustrated below.

Material price variance
Caused by changes in the purchase price of the materials used, and calculated by using the formula:

Actual quantity × Change in price

The change in price is the standard minus the actual price.

Material usage variance
Caused by changes in the quantity of materials used, and calculated by using the formula:

Standard price × Change in usage

The change in usage is the standard minus the actual usage.

Example 22
The standard material price and usage cost is 20m of material @ £8 a metre = £160 per unit.
The actual cost is 2,400m of material @ £7.60 a metre = £18,240 per 100 units

= £182.40 per unit.

The material price variance is = £960 favourable.
2,400 × (£8 − £7.60)

The material price is favourable because the price has fallen from £8 a metre to £7.60 a metre.

The material usage variance is = £3,200 adverse
£8 × (2,000 − 2,400)

The material usage variance is adverse because the usage has increased from 2,000m to 2,400m. This enables the total materials variance to be calculated from the £960 favourable variance and the £3,200 adverse variance, giving a net variance of £2,240 adverse. Comparing the actual material cost of £18,240 with the expected material cost of £16,000 (2,000m × £8 a metre) confirms the total material variance of £2,240 adverse, and shows the calculation of the individual material variances to be correct.

TROUBLESHOOTING AND CORRECTIVE ACTION

Having calculated the variances and found them to be outside the parameters that are acceptable to the organisation, the information system should flag them in some distinctive way so that the person responsible is made aware that action is necessary. Possible causes and suggested actions to correct the labour and material variances include:

Labour rate variance

- bad estimate – accept as an explainable variance until a new standard can be set

- nationally agreed change in wage rates – accept until a new standard can be set

- the employment of more or less highly skilled people than are needed to carry out the operation – make the necessary change to the personnel carrying out the work, and discuss with the supervisor/manager.

Labour efficiency variance

- bad estimate – accept until the standard can be changed

- the employment of more or less highly skilled people than planned for – make the necessary changes and have discussions with those responsible

- poor morale among staff – this is a serious problem for the personnel department, who will have to discover the cause and if possible rectify it; failing all else, people may have to be asked to leave.

Material price variance

- bad estimate – accept until the standard can be changed

- internationally agreed price change – accept until the standard can be changed

- the use of material of a better or worse quality than needed – make the necessary change in the material used and investigate with the purchasing section.

Material usage variance

- bad estimate – accept until the standard can be changed

- poor quality of material – investigate with purchasing section and take necessary action

- labour efficiency wastage of material – explore with the personnel department and correct as quickly as possible.

A good system of standard costing is invaluable to management in helping to ensure that an organisation is adhering to its planned course and that things are not getting out of control. A personnel manager who understands costing will not only be able better to control the costs of his or her department and demonstrate its effective management, but will also be able to assist in other areas, especially where variances in labour costs can be attributed to a mismatch between people's skills and their functions.

Work through Exercises 12 to 14 and compare your answers with the sample ones given at the back of the book.

Exercise 12
A service organisation has the following standard costs per day for the service it provides:

• labour, 8 hours @ £40 per hour

• materials, 5 litres @ £15 per litre

• overheads, £60 per day.

The actual costs for one week of five days are:

• labour, 38 hours @ £41 per hour

• materials, 28 litres @ £14.50 per litre

• overheads, £340.

Calculate the variances and comment on their use.

Exercise 13
The personnel department is responsible for providing a one-week 40-hour induction programme for new recruits. The standard costs of the programme are:

• hourly salary per recruit, £7.20

• hourly salary per trainer, £8.65

• overhead costs per week for the personnel department, £1,000.

The actual costs of a training week for 20 delegates are:

42 hours' training for 20 delegates with salaries of £7 per hour	£5880.00
42 hours' training by two trainers with salaries of £8.70 per hour	730.80
Overheads	1,200.00
	£7,810.80

Calculate the relevant variances and comment on their use to the personnel manager.

Exercise 14
Explain the main factors of standard costing that make it an effective control tool for personnel managers.

How are standard costs set?

What is a favourable variance?

What is the effect of a perfect standard on staff?

Why is it important to take corrective action when variances occur?

How could standard costing be used by the personnel manager to motivate staff in your organisation?

12 Marginal costing and personnel decisions

At the end of this chapter the reader should be able to use marginal costing in decision-making and relate it to the work of the personnel manager. The management competences that this chapter is intended to develop are those of making recommendations for expenditure and evaluating proposals for expenditure.

We have so far been concerned with ensuring that all costs are accounted for and recovered. There is also an approach to costing that focuses attention on those costs that will be altered by a particular decision, in order to emphasise the impact of the decision. This approach is called 'marginal costing', and although it is not a complete system it is of enormous help to the personnel manager when making decisions – for example, about selling, training or consultancy services (whether within or outside the organisation).

Under marginal costing the fixed costs – like depreciation, salaries and interest charges – are considered to have been set as a matter of policy and to remain fixed within given parameters for the period under review. This is not to say that the fixed costs are not important. For most undertakings they contribute the bulk of the costs incurred and to ignore them completely would be a recipe for disaster. But they can be regarded as not directly affecting a decision that is being made. The marginal cost can be described as the cost of one more unit, whether it is a product or a service, and the difference between these two costs is graphically illustrated in Figures 11 and 12.

Figure 11 **Marginal cost**

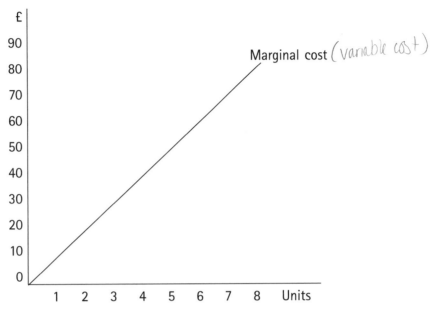

Figure 12 **Fixed cost**

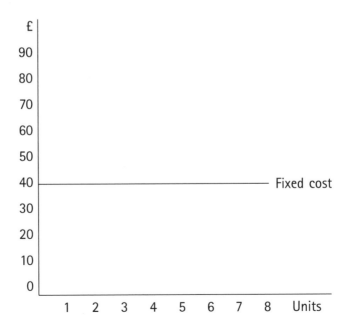

The marginal cost line starts at zero because if nothing is being done – no service provided or units made – no marginal cost is being incurred, whereas the fixed cost line is parallel to the base because the cost is the same whether one unit or eight units of product or service is being provided.

Marginal costing involves the important concept of contribution. Contribution is the selling price per unit of service or product minus the marginal cost per unit of providing it. The contribution goes first towards meeting the fixed costs of the organisation and then, provided the contribution is large enough, it becomes profit. If the contribution is not sufficient to meet the fixed costs, a loss is incurred.

Example 23
The personnel department offers training, for which it charges £100 per hour, for up to 20 delegates. The marginal costs have been calculated at £70 per hour and the fixed costs for the period are £9,990. The manager needs to know the contribution per hour, how many hours of training must be sold to break even (ie make neither a profit nor a loss), and what the profit or loss would be if 350 hours of training were sold.

The contribution per hour is the selling price per hour minus the marginal cost per hour:

$$£100 - £70 = £30$$

The number of hours that must be sold in order to break even is:

$$\frac{\text{Fixed costs}}{\text{Contribution per hour}} = \frac{£9,990}{30} = 333 \text{ hours}$$

The profit or loss if 350 hours of training are sold is the total contribution minus the fixed costs:

$$£10,500 \ (£30 \times 350 \text{ hours}) - £9,990 = £510$$

Let us look at another example of how this concept is used.

Example 24

A personnel consultancy organisation has fixed costs of £60,000, marginal costs of £50 per unit, and a selling-price of £150 per unit. Each unit that is sold contributes £100 to the fixed costs, and once these have been met the contribution is to profit. This can be further shown as:

Units sold	Contribution (£)	Fixed costs (£)	Profit (or loss) (£)
0	0	60,000	(60,000)
1	100	60,000	(59,900)
2	200	60,000	(59,800)
3	300	60,000	(59,700)
599	59,900	60,000	(100)
600	60,000	60,000	(0) break even
601	60,100	60,000	100

At 600 units the organisation breaks even. Sales of more than 600 units result in a profit, and less in a loss. The break-even point in units sold can be calculated by applying the formula:

$$\frac{\text{Total fixed costs}}{\text{Selling price} - \text{marginal cost per unit}}$$
$$\text{(contribution per unit)}$$

which in our example gives:

$$\frac{60,000}{(150 - 50)} = \frac{60,000}{100} = 600 \text{ units}$$

The relationship may be shown graphically (see Figure 13) if we assume the information previously given applies and the maximum possible number of units that can be sold is 700.

The horizontal axis represents activity – in this case the units sold – and the vertical axis value in terms of both costs and revenue. The horizontal axis goes to the maximum possible level of activity, and at this point a vertical line is drawn, which shows where all the lines of the graph end. The vertical axis must go up to the total sales or the total costs,

Figure 13 **Break-even point**

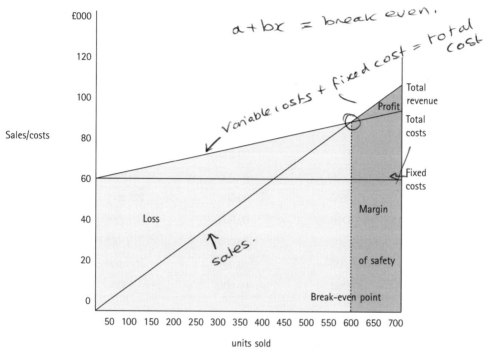

whichever is the greater. The total revenue is obtained by multiplying the total units sold by the selling-price per unit:

$$700 \times 150 = £105,000$$

A mark is made on the vertical line opposite the £105,000. This is then joined to the zero to give the total revenue line. The total cost is calculated by adding the fixed cost to the total marginal cost, which in this case is:

(marginal cost per unit × units sold) + fixed costs = (£50 × 700) + £60,000 = £35,000 + £60,000 = £95,000

A mark is made on the vertical axis opposite the £95,000 and joined to the fixed costs of £60,000 to give the total cost line. The break-even point is where the total cost and total revenue lines intercept. Anything to the left of it represents loss; anything to the right of it, profit.

Contribution is used by many organisations in an attempt to

ensure that spare capacity is fully employed at off-peak times. Rail and bus companies, British Telecom, the electricity utilities, British Airways and hotel chains are among those that have high fixed costs and employ a two- or multi-tier pricing system in order to persuade the public to use their services at off-peak times. Every extra contribution that is received helps to meet the enormous fixed costs they carry and either reduces losses or increases profits. Full rates are charged at peak periods but at off-peak times bargain offers are made. For example, South-West Trains charges approximately £30 return from Portsmouth to Waterloo at peak times but reduces it to £15.70 at off-peak times. Provided they are receiving more in fares than it is costing to run the train, they are receiving a contribution to their large fixed costs.

We have seen that there are several costing methods available to the personnel manager. The one you choose should meet your needs and provide you with relevant information to manage yourself and your department more effectively. Decisions based on incomplete or inappropriate information are bad decisions. To be successful, it is essential to have the right information in the right place at the right time.

Exercise 15
Look at Example 23. What would you recommend should be done if demand for training fell to 300 hours? What would be the magnitude of the loss?

Exercise 16
The personnel department markets its services in recruitment consultancy. The marginal cost has been calculated to be £19,500 per managerial appointment and the charge to the customers is £25,000 per appointment. The relevant fixed costs are £319,000, and it is expected that 70 managerial recruitments will be undertaken for clients. Draw the break-even chart for the above information and read from the chart the results of the planned 70 recruits.

Exercise 17
Enumerate three ways in which the concept of contribution is of help to personnel managers.

Exercise 18

Your managing director is reviewing training costs with a view to possibly purchasing training from consultants rather than employing your department. The costs of buying in training for the standard induction programme would be £4,000 for up to 20 delegates. The costs charged by your department are £6,000 for up to 20 delegates. The overheads charged to the department from head office are £10,000 and they are recovered in the quoted costs over four programmes. How would you demonstrate to the managing director that your department's costs are lower than those of the outside consultant?

What is the marginal cost?

How is contribution calculated?

What are fixed costs?

How is the break-even point calculated?

Investigate the application of marginal costing to the personnel function in your organisation.

13 The personnel manager and the planning system

At the end of this chapter the reader should understand the planning process and its application to the organisation as well as to the personnel department. The management competences that this chapter is intended to develop are those of controlling expenditure against budgets, reviewing the generation and allocation of financial resources, and obtaining financial resources for your organisation's activities.

A chart of the planning system is shown in Figure 14.

Figure 14 **A planning system**

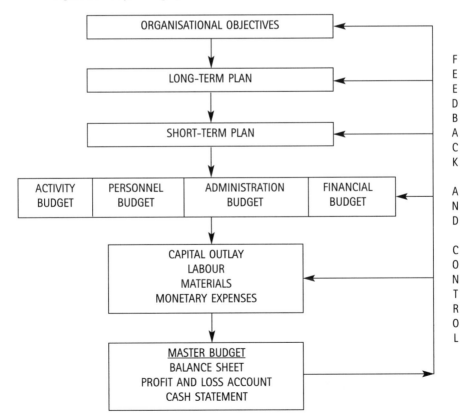

In following this model we see that the first purpose of the planning system is to ensure that organisational objectives are set. This is usually undertaken by the top executives who would normally include the chief executive together with his or her deputy, the personnel director, the financial director and the marketing director. Other people may be co-opted onto the team as they are required, but it is usual to keep the group to a workable size whenever possible. In setting the objectives the team will have regard to the past performance of the organisation, particularly over the last two or three years, as well as the likely events of the next five years or so that will have an impact on it. In doing this they will consider reports from people who are in touch with the customers so that any changes in customer profile can be quickly identified. The latest economic forecasts will be considered, together with population trends and expected changes in fashion and technology. There are a great many different organisational objectives that might be set, including such things as providing the fastest service, being most concerned about the environment, having the largest market share, having the happiest employees, making the biggest profit, or making the most reliable product.

The objectives may be for up to 10 years ahead, but it is important to remember that they are subject to change. No undertaking survives for long in the current highly competitive environment unless it is able to respond quickly and effectively to changing conditions, but objectives do set a course that the organisation is able to follow.

LONG-TERM PLAN

This is drawn up to enable the objectives to be achieved and will probably cover the next 10 years, but it is important to remember that it is virtually impossible to plan accurately so far into the future. The first year will be relatively firm, and years two and three should be fairly accurate unless something unexpected occurs, like 'Black Monday' in October 1987 when the stock market collapsed. Years four and five will be rather less certain, and years six to 10 pretty tentative, except perhaps in the case of large projects which require extensive capital outlay. The long-term plan will be adjusted year by year as a result of feedback as to its feasibility, once it has been expressed in financial terms in the master budget. In particular during its early years, it will be the subject of a great deal of in-fighting as each manager stakes a claim for as large a share of the budget 'cake' as possible. Personalities will be very much to the fore, and there is a real danger that unless there is a good system with a reasonable approach, the most aggressive character will receive far more than his or her entitlement. It is important that the personnel manager should make a good case – otherwise, the department will suffer.

SHORT-TERM PLAN

This will be the budget for the next twelve months, and before it is finished consultation will ideally have taken place at all levels of the concern. Without the opportunity to be involved in the preparation of the budget, people will feel that it has been imposed on them and be resentful. If, on the other hand, they feel that they have contributed to its preparation, they are more likely to feel involved and supportive, so that the chances of the plan being adhered to will be greatly enhanced.

The budget works in the same way as standard costing, the difference being in scale. Whereas standard costing refers to a job, operation, section or department, budgetary control encompasses the whole organisation, but uses exactly the same technique as standard costing. Actual performance is compared with planned performances on a weekly, monthly or quarterly basis, and significant differences are reported upon so that corrective action can be taken. The behavioural impact of the system is extremely important because it can have a major effect on the way people behave.

THE BUDGETS

The short-term plan feeds into the detailed budgets discussed below, which are firm for the first year but become more tentative the further they go into the future. With all planning it is important to be flexible and to allow for the unexpected, because things will change, and attempts to treat a budget as set in tablets of stone, under no circumstances to be altered, will cause more problems than they solve.

Activity budget
This consists of the expected hours of service that an organisation believes it can provide in the period that is being planned for, or units it can produce, or jobs it can complete. It will be based on the information – provided by market research carried out by the undertaking's employees, or bought in – as to the likely level of demand. The information will have to be handled with care, for there is a danger that people will want to paint an optimistic picture and may unintentionally overstate the level of demand. To counteract this it is a good idea to obtain information from as many sources as possible and to prepare three levels of activity: most pessimistic, most optimistic and most likely. This will help to minimise the risk of people's getting carried away with their own enthusiasm.

Having set the budget, it is essential to monitor it closely to ensure that errors are quickly noticed and the relevant corrections made. Bad planning here will have an impact throughout the whole concern, as will be discussed later in this chapter.

Personnel budget
In order to meet the level of demand anticipated by the activity budget, it is essential to ensure that enough people of the right calibre are available throughout the organisation. To achieve this, effective recruitment systems have to be in place, reinforced by job analysis and training programmes. It is fashionable and necessary for both the public and private sectors to be lean and healthy, and for them to succeed people must operate effectively.

The fast-changing environment in which we all operate means that people must be flexible in their approach and constantly retrained to keep up with current developments. The personnel manager has a key role in ensuring that the requirements of staff for development are identified and met. Failure to achieve this will lead first to a demotivated team because staff feel that they are not performing effectively, and then to the possible demise of the organisation because it fails to compete with more efficient concerns.

Administration budget

Built around the expected level of activity, this budget will ensure that the correct administrative systems are in place with suitably experienced and/or qualified people to enable the organisation to meet the demands that are placed upon it. Obtaining the right person to meet the particular needs of a section or department is an extremely specialised matter, and recruitment consultants are frequently called in, particularly for the more senior positions. Good administration can help ensure the successful implementation of plans, so this budget should be capable of providing the necessary resources to meet the concern's needs.

Financial budget

The financial budget is based on the activity budget and is used to ensure that there are sufficient financial resources for the plan to be met. Undertakings need resources of materials, labour and money to enable them to operate, and a shortage of any one of these will cause plans to fail. Finance is used in every area, as are people and materials, but there is a danger that the financial implications of plans or actions may sometimes be overlooked. The preparation of the financial budget helps to ensure that this does not happen, because every manager is involved and the accountant's role, contrary to popular belief, is simply to clothe their ideas in monetary terms.

In the past some accountants have been seen as unapproachable people, speaking a strange language, whose main purpose in life was to say no, closely followed by a desire to confuse. This is now changing, and the accountant is perceived more as an organisational resource, a person who can give valuable advice on a great many matters.

Capital outlay budget

Capital outlay involves heavy expenditure on such fixed assets as land and buildings, plant and machinery, or fixtures and fittings, which may be spent in one year, but may also involve large capital programmes spread over several years. Examples would be a new housing estate, a land reclamation scheme, a drainage system, a sports complex, or the development of a commercial dock. The capital budget, unlike the revenue budgets, often involves heavy expenditure spread over several years and should therefore receive close scrutiny before any schemes are finally approved. Various methods are available, and they are described in Chapter 16.

Materials budget

This is prepared in order to ensure that sufficient materials are available to meet the anticipated demand, while at the same time enabling the undertaking to avoid tying up too much money in unnecessarily high stocks of material. The level will depend on the forecast in the activity budget, but it should be borne in mind that more and more organisations are attempting to use the 'just-in-time' method of inventory control. In practice it is extremely difficult to achieve, and because so much depends on the reliability of the supplier, any small delay causing enormous problems.

Cash budget

This is a more sensitive version of the financial budget which concentrates on the day-to-day movements of money in the concern. It is complementary to the financial budget, and draws on the activity and other budgets. Properly monitored, the cash budget can be extremely helpful in controlling the activities of the organisation and avoiding embarrassing short-term cash-flow problems. Many chief executives ensure that surplus cash is invested on the money market overnight to earn interest. The subject is dealt with in Chapter 14.

Expenses budget

This covers the expected level of such items of expense as rates, heating and lighting, telephones, postage, stationery and canteen costs. Most of them will be known with a reasonable degree of certainty, at least for the next year, and, although they have to be integrated with the other budgets, they are not so directly affected by differing levels of activity.

Master budget

The master budget clothes these ideas in monetary terms to see whether they are in fact feasible when measured against planned levels of profitability and liquidity. If it shows that there will be a loss instead of a profit, or that too little money will be generated, the information will be fed back into the system and the process restarted.

None of the budgets mentioned can stand on its own, and each depends on the others. It is no use planning to provide 10,000 hours of service if you only have enough people to give 7,000 hours, or to produce 50,000 units if you are only able to sell 40,000. To avoid mismatching of this sort, organisations have to decide what their limiting factor is – that is to say, which of the budgets is most restricted, either through shortage of resources or because of a lack of demand. Once identified, the limiting factor becomes the starting-point of the budget, and all the others are built around it. An undertaking may decide that it can meet any level of demand, and if this is so, then the activity or sales budget will be the starting-point and all the other budgets will be dependent on it, as illustrated in Figure 15. This shows an integrated system of budgeting in which each budget has an impact on the others, but the one that restricts the overall budgets, in this case, is the activity/sales budget.

Figure 15 Limiting factor activity/sales budget

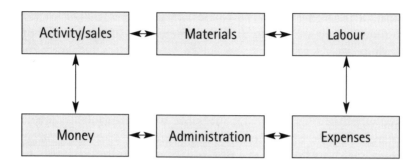

The system is as appropriate for the public sector as it is for the private sector, but the limiting factor in the public sector is frequently money and so a more apt model for the sector would be as in Figure 16.

Figure 16 Limiting factor cash budget

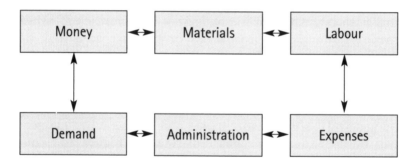

Exercise 19

An organisation has budgeted sales for three months (twelve weeks) of 600 units at £20 each. The material bought and used will be 300 pounds (weight) at 60p a pound. The labour cost will be 360 hours at £15 per hour, and other expenses £40 per week. The cash in hand at the start of the period is £400. Customers receive one month's credit, and suppliers and other expenses are paid on time. Draw up the sales, materials, labour, expenses and cash budgets for the three months and the budgeted profit and loss account and balance sheet. No money is due from customers. At the beginning of the three months, there is 10 pounds (weight) of material in hand and £406 capital.

What are the three parts of the master budget?

What is the limiting factor?

How does the planning system impact on people's behaviour?

Why should the personnel manager be involved in the process?

Prepare a model of your organisation's planning system and compare it with the one illustrated in this chapter. What do you consider to be its strengths and weaknesses? What is the personnel manager's contribution to the planning system? Identify the main items of income and expenditure for which he or she is responsible.

Draw up the plan or budget for the personnel department for the coming year. If you do not know how much money will be involved for each item, simply list the headings involved.

14 The cash budget

At the end of this chapter the reader should understand the cash budget and the way in which a personnel manager would use it in order to control the cash resources of the personnel department. The management competences that this chapter is intended to develop are those of controlling expenditure against budgets, obtaining financial resources for your organisation's activities and reviewing the generation and allocation of financial resources.

As we saw in Chapter 13, the cash budget is used to plan and control the cash balances on a day-to-day basis. Money, like the other resources employed in organisations, is costly and should not be allowed to sit around doing nothing. It should be continuously working, and to have too much is as bad as having too little. The working capital is derived by taking the current liabilities away from the current assets of the undertaking, and is used to pay the running costs until more money is earned. The overall measure of a concern's liquidity and of its ability to pay its way is the amount of money it has readily available, which is generally represented by the cash in hand and cash at bank.

In drawing up the cash budget the only figure that is known with absolute certainty is the opening balance, which is the amount of money that is in hand or overdrawn at the start of the budget period. The rest of the items are largely estimates, or informed guesses, based on past experience and taking into account present and expected conditions. The receipts from the sale of goods, or the number of hours' service provided, or rent for accommodation, will rarely be what is due or has been earned, but will rather be what has been earned minus late receipts of cash. For example, in a particular month a local authority may have charged rates of £70,000 but the payments received might be only £50,000. This sort of difference between what should be received and what is actually received should be catered for in the cash budget.

The same technique should be applied item by item, and those responsible for drawing up the budget should always remember that things will rarely happen exactly as they are planned. The government, with some of the best brains in the world at its disposal, was unable to get its forecast right when it launched the BP flotation, so ordinary mortals should not be too despondent when their plans go awry. Constant monitoring keeps any problems to a minimum.

Payments by organisations to their suppliers are just as likely to be delayed as receipts from customers, and it should be remembered that, within reasonable limits, accounts departments control when they make payments, whereas they do not have nearly so much control over when monies are received. Purchases may be paid for anything up to three months after the goods have been received, and some concerns wait even longer than that. The danger is that suppliers will become so tired of waiting for their money that any further goods are supplied on a cash-only basis or, what is perhaps worse, rumours will circulate that the organisation is having cash-flow problems and people refuse to deal with it at all. An extreme example of delayed payment would be purchases for one month £20,000, payments for purchases £0, but this generally occurs only in the very early months of an undertaking, or when it is undergoing some sort of restructuring or other problem. More usually the figures would be something like purchases £20,000, payments £12,000.

The illustration of a cash budget in Example 25 is not meant to be comprehensive but it does include many of the items more usually encountered. Once you have studied it, use a similar structure to solve Exercise 20.

The budget shows a cash deficit of £12,000 at the end of December, but it should not cause too great a problem: if the cash budget has been closely monitored, the accountant will be aware of it in plenty of time to arrange an overdraft facility with the bank or other financing. If that proves impossible, it may be feasible to delay some of the capital expenditure. Or if none of these solutions is possible, the business could be sold as a going concern before things got out of hand. Each month the actual position is compared with the plan, and to be useful, the information must be available within at least a week of the month-end, and sooner than that if possible. Many undertakings monitor their cash on a daily basis and employ a computerised information system to enable them to do so. Any surplus monies are invested on the overnight market.

Let us now apply the techniques of the cash budget to the role of the personnel manager. The personnel department is generally treated as a cost centre which provides little financial benefit to the organisation. We have seen that this view can be challenged by an efficient personnel manager not only on the grounds of monies generated by selling training and recruitment facilities to outside organisations but also by demonstrating the savings that accrue when properly recruited and trained staff are working effectively. Indeed, it might be argued that the personnel department is a profit centre rather than a cost centre.

The cash budget for a personnel department utilises exactly the same principles as those already described, although the headings might be slightly different. Such a cash budget might look like Example 26.

Example 25

Cash budget for three months to 31 December

	October		November		December	
	Plan	*Actual*	*Plan*	*Actual*	*Plan*	*Actual*
Opening balance in hand			£59,000		£27,000	
(overdrawn)	(£4,000)					
Receipts from sales:						
this month	80,000		90,000		88,000	
previous month	104,000		120,000		130,000	
Total	£180,000		£269,000		£245,000	
Less Payments for goods						
this month	40,000		45,000		60,000	
previous month	50,000		60,000		70,000	
Wages and salaries	20,000		20,000		20,000	
Heating and lighting	–		–		4,000	
Transport	5,000		10,000		15,000	
Rates					10,000	
Capital items:						
Purchase of fixed assets	–		100,000		50,000	
Postage and stationery	2,000		1,000		2,000	
Telephones	3,000		4,000		5,000	
Loan interest	–		–		20,000	
Miscellaneous	1,000		2,000		1,000	
Total	121,000		242,000		257,000	
Balance c/f in hand						
(overdrawn)	£59,000		£27,000		(£12,000)	

Example 26

	January		February		March	
	Plan	*Actual*	*Plan*	*Actual*	*Plan*	*Actual*
Opening balance						
Receipts:						
Training						
Recruitment						
Payments:						
Employees						
Training						
Recruitment						
Travelling						
Materials						
Business rate						
Electricity						
Postage						
Telephone						
Services						
Capital						
Miscellaneous						
Total						
Balance c/f						

By comparing the planned with the actual activity on a monthly basis, the personnel manager can ensure that effective corrective action is taken. Estimates of payments are generally easier to make accurately than estimates of income, although with practice both will improve.

Exercise 20

Peter Brown intends to make and sell wooden models of famous sports personalities. Each model takes eight hours to make. Brown charges £8 per hour for his labour and uses mahogany costing £30; he adds 50% to the cost price to arrive at his selling-price and feels that there is a market for his product. Research has made him believe that once he is established and his product becomes known, he will be able to sell 10 models a week, and he would like to maintain a buffer stock of three of the most popular models. He gives four weeks' credit and anticipates the demand to be: weeks 1 to 3, no sales; weeks 4 and 5, six sales; week 6 onwards, 10 sales. His other costs will be rent of a shed, £10 per week; postage and stationery, £231 per week; rates, electricity and telephone, £1,200 per quarter, paid in March, June, September and December. The wood is purchased and paid for monthly in advance, with enough for 40 models, and stored on racks in the shed. Brown has brought in £10,000 as capital, and he has bought equipment for £8,000, leaving a cash balance of £2,000. The business is to start on 1 January. Draw up the cash budget for the six months January to June, assuming that Brown withdraws £200 per week for living expenses and pays for additional equipment costing £5,000 in June. Would you recommend Brown to start the business? (NB Treat each month as four weeks.)

Exercise 21

Draw up the cash budget from the following information for the six months from 1 July to 31 December.

• Opening cash balance at 1 July: £3,000

• Sales at £40 per unit

	April	May	June	July	Aug	Sept	Oct	Nov	Dec
units	220	240	280	320	360	380	260	160	140

- Payment for goods two months after they have been sold

- £10 per unit direct labour payable in the same month as production

- Raw materials cost £12 per unit, paid for three months after the goods are used in production

- Production in units:

	April	May	June	July	Aug	Sept	Oct	Nov	Dec	Jan
units	300	340	360	400	260	220	200	180	140	120

- Other variable expenses are £6 per unit; two-thirds of this cost is paid for in the same month as production and one-third in the month following production

- Fixed expenses of £300 per month, paid one month in arrears

- Capital expenditure for September: £20,000.

Exercise 22

The balance sheet of Dave's Delicatessen at 31 October

Premises	£10,000			Capital	£13,750
Depreciation	2,000			Creditors	3,000
		£8,000		Overdraft	1,050
Fittings	8,000				
Depreciation	4,000	4,000			
Stock		5,000			
Debtors		800			
		17,800			17,800

- Sales are budgeted to be

November	December	January	February	March	April
£6,000	£10,000	£7,000	£23,000	£4,000	£8,000

- Some sales are on credit and the proportions are on average 10 per cent credit, 90 per cent cash; credit customers pay in the month following the sales

- The gross profit margin is 25 per cent of selling-price

- Stocks are maintained at a constant level throughout the year

- Fifty per cent of purchases are paid for in the same month as they are purchased and 50 per cent in the subsequent month

- Wages and other running expenses are £2,000 per month paid in the month in which they are incurred

- Premises and fittings are depreciated at 10 per cent per annum on cost.

Prepare a cash budget showing Dave's bank balance or overdraft for each month in the half-year ending 30 April.

Why is the cash budget important?

What is liquidity measured by?

Why should corrective action be taken quickly when actual figures differ from the budget?

Why is it usually easier to estimate expenditure than to estimate cash receipts?

Prepare a cash budget for your department. Discuss the figures that you arrive at with the personnel manager and/or the accountant.

15 The master budget

At the end of this chapter the reader should understand the preparation of the master budget and its links with the other budgets of the concern. The management competencies that this chapter is intended to develop are those of reviewing the generation and allocation of financial resources and controlling expenditure against budgets.

The master budget consists of the forecast trading and profit and loss account, revenue account, balance sheet and cash statement. It draws on all the other budgets and can be completed only after they have been prepared. The budgeting process is a long-drawn-out affair which takes up to nine months, and there are usually several attempts before the plan is finally agreed. There is a danger that people will become cynical about the process because they may have observed over the years, for example, that, whatever is set as the first budget, it is returned with a request that it should be pruned by 15 per cent. This makes them inflate the original plan by 15 per cent in the expectation that when the negotiations are completed they will receive the budget allocation they feel is necessary to allow them to function effectively.

Most budgets are set by looking at what has happened in the past and then adding whatever is necessary to keep up with inflation and extra needs. This has the adverse effect of making people spend up to budget in the last month or two of a year, because they fear that any unspent money will be lost and as a consequence the budget for the next year will be reduced. Zero-based budgeting has been introduced as a means of avoiding this. This approach looks at the future needs of each budget centre and ignores anything that has happened in the past. The budget centre – which may be a branch, a department, a section or a product – is asked to submit its plan, and this is compared with requests from all the other budget centres before a decision is made. It is believed that this avoids the rush to spend up to budget before the year-end, and so saves money, although it is a more time-consuming approach.

The negotiation inevitably involved means that the master budget has to be prepared several times before the process is complete because the original plans may lead to a shortage of cash or a loss instead of a profit, and this information will be fed back into the system as illustrated in Figure 14 on page 113, allowing the necessary revision to be made. The master budget enables the results of the planned activities to be expressed in the international language of finance, and provides a concise overall picture of the situation that can be readily assimilated and discussed by those concerned.

We have already seen that the budget for the personnel department is an integral part of this process. The personnel manager will have consulted with his or her staff to ascertain the likely level of activity over the forthcoming year for all aspects of the department's functions. Ideally, these plans will have been fully discussed within the department before they are finally submitted to the budget committee. If the department is to function effectively, it is essential for all members to be fully committed to its objectives as stated in the budget, and the best way to obtain this commitment is through involvement – ownership is important.

Different departmental managers have different approaches to the process, and a great deal depends on the character of the individual involved. There is a danger in constantly asking for more or less than you require in order to run your department effectively in that you may well lose the respect of your colleagues. The manager who in the long term gains most from the negotiations is the one who makes careful estimates of future activities based on the information available at the time. There will of course be mistakes, but as long as they are seen and corrected early enough, no major damage will be done.

Let us now consider the master budget of a manufacturing concern. The process followed is that illustrated in the model system in Chapter 13. We will first show the budget and then explain how each of the individual items has been derived. This will be followed by the budget of a public authority.

Example 27

Forecast manufacturing account of Makes Co. for the year ending 30 June

	£	£
Opening inventory of raw materials		40,000
Add Raw materials purchased		810,000
		850,000
Deduct Closing inventory of raw materials		60,000
Raw materials consumed		790,000
Direct manufacturing wages		1,410,000
Direct expenses		10,000
Prime/direct cost of goods made		2,210,000
Add Indirect factory expenses/overheads:		
Salaries and wages	70,000	
Materials	30,000	
Heating and lighting	40,000	
Rent and rates	60,000	
Depreciation	90,000	
		290,000
Total manufacturing cost		2,500,000
Add Opening work in progress		10,000
		2,510,000
Deduct Closing work in progress		20,000
Cost of finished goods made		2,490,000

Forecast trading and profit and loss account of Makes Co. for the year ending 30 June

	£	£
Sales		7,600,000
Less Cost of goods sold:		
Opening inventory of finished goods	40,000	
Add Cost of goods manufactured	2,490,000	
	2,530,000	
Deduct Closing inventory of finished goods	30,000	
		2,500,000
Gross profit		5,100,000
Less Expenses:		
Wages and salaries	3,750,000	
Selling and distribution	250,000	
Heating and lighting	40,000	
Depreciation	120,000	
Financing charges	65,000	
Miscellaneous	15,000	
		4,240,000
Net profit before tax		860,000

Forecast balance sheet of Makes Co. as at 30 June

	£	£		£	£
Land and buildings	5,400,000		Capital		2,810,000
Less depreciation	2,300,000		Reserves		2,320,000
		3,100,000	Loans		500,000
Plant and machinery	1,960,000				
Less depreciation	660,000				
		1,300,000			
Motor vehicles	320,000				
Less depreciation	60,000				
		260,000			
Current assets:			Current liabilities:		
Inventory of raw materials	60,000		Creditors	70,000	
Inventory of work in progress	20,000		Accruals	20,000	
Inventory of finished goods	30,000				90,000
	110,000				
Debtors	940,000				
Bank	10,000				
		1,060,000			
		5,720,000			5,720,000

Budget relationships

Opening inventory of raw materials ⎫	
Raw materials purchased ⎬	Materials budget
Closing inventory of raw materials ⎭	
Direct manufacturing wages	Labour budget
Direct expenses	Expenses budget
Salaries and wages	Labour budget
Materials ⎫	
Heating and lighting ⎬	Expenses budget
Rent and rates ⎭	
Depreciation	Capital assets budget
Work in progress	
Opening ⎫	
Closing ⎭	Materials budget
Sales	Activity budget
Opening inventory of finished goods ⎫	
Closing inventory of finished goods ⎭	Finished goods budget
Salaries and wages	Administration budget
Selling and distribution ⎫	Expenses budget
Heating and lighting ⎭	
Financing changes	Financial budget
Miscellaneous	Expenses budget
Land and buildings ⎫	
Plant and machinery ⎬	Capital assets budget
Motor vehicles	
Depreciation ⎭	
Inventory of raw materials ⎫	
Inventory of work in progress ⎭	Materials budget
Inventory of finished goods	Finished goods budget
Debtors	Activity budget
Bank	Cash budget
Capital	Master budget
Resources	Master budget
Loans	Financial budget
Creditors	Materials budget
Accruals	Expenses budget

GENERAL FUND SUMMARY

Including decisions made at City Council on 24 February 1998 – Spending at Standard Spending Assessment

Actual 1996/97 £	Original Estimate 1997/98 £	Revised Estimate 1997/98 £	NET REQUIREMENTS OF COMMITTEES	Estimate 1998/99 £
412,848	5,102,800	5,221,900	Crime Prevention and Public Safety	5,927,200
(18,676)	10,000	(9,800)	Licensing	(6,300)
2,465,392	5,643,600	5,670,200	Cultural and Heritage Services	5,767,800
1,708,358	1,706,460	1,813,700	Economic Development and International Relations	1,914,300
0	71,025,300	69,976,700	Education	77,475,700
5,868,948	8,764,500	9,206,100	Environment	9,902,100
4,252,944	6,314,020	5,681,600	Housing (General Fund)	7,005,500
10,263,178	11,170,600	11,214,800	Leisure and Community Services	11,766,200
2,294,612	2,571,020	2,515,600	Planning	2,716,800
			Policy & Resources	
(3,000,995)	(3,219,000)	(3,748,800)	Commercial Port Board	(3,750,000)
5,601,186	10,781,240	10,218,200	Resources Management	11,714,400
2,155,354	0	0	Unitary Sub Committee	0
0	33,730,000	34,444,800	Social Services	37,601,000
2,463,182	8,039,200	8,265,900	Traffic and Transportation	8,729,700
34,466,331	161,639,740	160,470,900		176,764,400
			COMMITTEE EXPENDITURE	
			OTHER EXPENDITURE/(INCOME)	
(62,849)	0	(192,500)	Insurance reserve – net (surplus)/deficit	20,000
73,637	65,000	65,000	Provision for doubtful debts	65,000
81,609	83,540	81,000	Precepts	85,100
0	155,300	155,300	Compensatory Added Years Payments	16,000
188,559	125,000	125,000	City Training/Portsmouth ITEC Externalisation	40,000
(31,742)	0	0	General Rates Surplus	0
0	848,000	103,300	Contingency	1,000,000
1,383,800	2,691,000	2,409,000	Revenue contributions to capital reserve	4,400,100
(8,508,051)	(17,188,130)	(19,500,000)	Asset Management Revenue Account surplus	(18,480,200)
(316,860)	0	0	Millennium Scheme – Capitalisation Direction Required	0
27,274,434	148,419,450	143,717,000	**TOTAL (NET) EXPENDITURE**	164,054,400
			FINANCED BY:	
1,921,562	2,345,450	(2,357,000)	Contribution from/(to) balances and reserves	7,727,641
14,620,875	72,515,187	72,515,187	Revenue Support Grant	78,344,947
6,693,987	42,886,761	42,886,761	Business Rate income	44,867,579
4,038,010	30,672,052	30,672,052	Collection Fund	33,114,233
27,274,434	148,419,450	143,717,000		164,054,400
			BALANCES & RESERVES	
8,881,697	4,845,450	6,960,135	Balance brought forward at 1 April	10,812,780
(1,921,562)	(2,345,450)	2,357,000	Deduct deficit for the year	(7,727,641)
6,960,135	2,500,000	9,317,135	Balance carried forward at 31 March	3,085,139
		1,495,645	Add transfer from HCC 31 March 1997	
		10,812,780		

GENERAL BALANCES & RESERVES

	General Balances £	Other £	TOTAL £
31 March 1997	6,950,513	9,622	6,960,135
Add from HCC	1,416,150	79,495	1,495,645
1 April 1997	8,366,663	89,117	8,455,780
Used 1997/98	2,359,000	(2,000)	2,357,000
31 March 1998	10,725,663	87,117	10,812,780
Used 1998/99	(7,725,641)	(2,000)	(7,727,641)
31 March 1999	3,000,022	85,117	3,085,139

SPECIFIC BALANCES/RESERVES

	Off-Street Parking £	Capital Reserve £	Port Board Reserve £
1 April 1997	591,000	1,383,800	0
Contributions 97/98	103,300	2,409,000	1,038,800
Used 1997/98	(601,100)	(2,632,120)	(225,000)
31 March 1998	93,200	1,160,680	813,800
Contributions 98/99	340,900	4,400,100	413,800
Used 1998/99	0	(1,736,470)	(181,000)
31 March 1999	434,100	3,824,310	1,046,600

Calculation of the Council Tax 1998/99

Portsmouth City Council	1998/99 £	1997/98 £
Gross Expenditure	310,453,986	316,815,598
LESS Gross Income	154,127,227	170,741,598
Net Expenditure 1998/89	156,326,759	146,074,000
LESS Revenue Support Grant/NDR Pool contribution	123,212,526	115,401,948
	33,114,233	30,672,052
ADD/(DEDUCT) Collection Fund Deficit (Surplus) at 31 March	(842,340)	(385,500)
Net Budget Requirement – Portsmouth City Council Purposes	32,271,893	30,286,552
Council Tax Base	55,234.0	54,932.5
Council Tax – Portsmouth City Council Purposes at Band D		

$$\frac{32,271,893}{55,234.0} =$$

	1998/99	1997/98
	584.28	551.34

	1998/99	1997/98
Hampshire Police Authority Precept	*2,768,880*	*2,842,757*
Council Tax – Hampshire Police Authority Purposes at Band D	50.13	51.75

*The Council Tax to be levied for all bands in 1998/99
will be as follows:*

Estimated Valuation at 1 April 1991	Band	Hampshire Police Authority £	Portsmouth City Council £	TOTAL £	1997/98 £
Up to £40,000	A	33.42	389.52	422.94	402.06
£40,001–£52,000	B	38.99	454.44	493.43	469.07
£52,001–£68,000	C	44.56	519.36	563.92	536.08
£68,001–£88,000	D	50.13	584.28	634.41	603.09
£88,001–£120,000	E	61.27	714.12	775.39	737.11
£120,001–£160,000	F	72.41	843.96	916.37	871.13
£160,001–£320,000	G	83.55	973.80	1,057.35	1,005.15
£320,000 and over	H	100.26	1,168,56	1,268.82	1,206.18

From these examples it can be seen that the budgetary control system is totally integrated and can be of use to the organization only as long as it remains so. If any one budget is made to stand on its own, the system becomes useless. The way in which the budget is drawn up from basic information is shown in Chapter 13, which should be further studied in conjunction with this chapter.

> What are the constituent parts of the master budget?
>
> How does the master budget link with the other budgets of an undertaking?
>
> How may the personnel manager influence the master budget?
>
> What will happen if the master budget reveals a situation that is disliked by the planning team?

> Discuss the master budget of your organisation with the accountant, and ascertain the process by which it is prepared.

16 Capital budgeting and its application to personnel

At the end of this chapter the reader should understand the process of capital budgeting and be able to use the pay-back accounting rate of return and discounted cash-flow techniques to justify proposed capital expenditure. The management competences that this chapter is intended to develop are those of making recommendations for expenditure and evaluating proposals for expenditure.

All systems of budgetary control are important and require the utmost care in their preparation and monitoring, but whereas revenue budgets commit an organisation for only a short period of time, normally one year, capital schemes can commit them to expenditure for 10 or more years. The capital budget of an undertaking in its original draft may be drawn up on similar lines to Example 28 (see page 137) for the next 10 years.

The budget committee would focus most strongly on years 1 and 2, but as concerns face more demands on their resources than can be met, some method of deciding which among competing schemes should go forward for further consideration has to be devised. It is important to emphasise that methods which help to eliminate some schemes do not make the decision – all they do is give the decision-maker additional information on which to act.

There are four generally accepted methods of 'capital rationing' that are of help in deciding which schemes should be allowed to go forward for further consideration: pay-back, rate of return, discounted cash-flow and cost-benefits analysis. Each of them is useful to the personnel manager who is making bids for money to invest in capital schemes.

PAY-BACK

This enables the time taken to recover the initial investment

Example 28

Project	Total £(000)	Year 1 £(000)	Year 2 £(000)	Year 3 £(000)	Year 4 £(000)	Year 5 £(000)	Year 6 £(000)	Year 7 £(000)	Year 8 £(000)	Year 9 £(000)	Year 10 £(000)
A	22,300	4,000	8,000	10,000	300						
B	22,290			400	900	7,500	12,800	690			
C	650	600	50								
D	16,000	12,500	2,500	1,000							
E	33,200	7,000	200	9,000	8,000	6,000	2,400	600			
F	24,000								4,000	8,000	12,000
G	43,700			7,000	15,000	20,000	1,200	500			
H	33,700		7,600	19,400	6,200	500					
I	8,000				8,000						
J	40	40							100		
K	10	10									
L	60	60									
M	15	15									
TOTAL	204,065	24,225	18,350	46,800	38,400	34,000	16,400	1,790	4,100	8,000	12,000

– either through additional money coming into the organisation or by reducing the cash outflow – to be calculated. The result can then be compared with the desired pay-back period, which might be three years. Schemes that meet the criterion – ie that have a pay-back of three years or less – go forward for consideration, whereas others are excluded. Example 29 shows such a system of pay-back.

Example 29
The personnel department requires a piece of machinery that costs £30,000 and is more efficient than the existing machine, resulting in an annual saving in operating cost, excluding depreciation, over five years of £6,000 in year 1, £8,000 in year 2 and £10,000 in years 3 to 5. The pay-back in this case, provided the savings are generated equally throughout the year, would be:

	£	£	£
Cost			30,000
Pay-back		*Cumulative*	
Year 1	6,000	6,000	
Year 2	8,000	14,000	
Year 3	10,000	24,000	
Year 4 (7.2 months)	6,000	30,000	

In this case pay-back takes three years and 7.2 months, so that if a three-year pay-back was the sole criterion, then the scheme would not go forward for further consideration.

Budget-holders are concerned with the speed at which their outlay is recovered, so this method of capital rationing is frequently used in practice. It is easy to understand and apply, but it has the disadvantage of ignoring what happens once pay-back has been achieved and does not review the scheme as a whole. On the other hand, it has the advantage of recognising, even if only indirectly, that money recovered earlier is more valuable than money received later, because money that you have can be invested and earn interest.

ACCOUNTING RATE OF RETURN

The accounting rate of return is calculated by expressing the average annual cash-flow generated by the scheme as a percentage of the outlay.

Applying the cash-flow shown in Example 29, we have:

$$\text{Outlay} \qquad £30,000$$

Average annual cash flows:

$$\frac{£6,000 + £8,000 + £10,000 + £10,000 + £10,000}{5 \text{ years}}$$

$$= \quad \frac{£44,000}{5}$$

$$= \quad £8,800 \text{ per annum}$$

The average annual cash flow of £8,800 is then expressed as a percentage of the outlay of £30,000:

$$= \quad \frac{£8,800 \times 100}{£30,000} \quad = 29.3\%$$

If the organisation was looking for a return of 30 per cent, this scheme would be excluded, but if 25 per cent was the required rate, it would go forward for further consideration. This method is not as commonly employed as the pay-back, although it is relatively easy to understand and apply and it does review the whole scheme. Its disadvantage is that it ignores the time-value of money – that is, £1 received today is treated as having the same value as £1 received in 10 years' time, which is nonsense in view of the opportunities of investing the money available now.

DISCOUNTED CASH-FLOW (NET PRESENT VALUE)

This approach is considered to be superior to both pay-back and accounting rate of return because it considers both the true value of money and the whole life of the scheme. The basis of the approach is that if you have a pound (sterling) today, you can invest it and earn interest at, say, 6 per cent. If, on the other hand, you have to wait a year before you receive the pound, you have lost the opportunity to earn a year's interest. In view of this, the pound that you have today is more valuable than a pound that you are going to receive at some time in the future. There is a discount table that you can employ to reflect this difference in value, and tables for 8 per cent, 15 per cent and 16 per cent discount rates are shown in the Appendix at the end of the book, but tables are available for all the discount rates that are likely to be required.

Applying discounted cash-flow techniques to arrive at the net present value of the scheme, and assuming that the organisation requires a 16 per cent return on investment, we have:

Outlay		£30,000

Savings:

Year 1	£6,000 × 0.8621 = 5172.6	
Year 2	£8,000 × 0.7432 = 5945.6	
Year 3	£10,000 × 0.6407 = 6407	
Year 4	£10,000 × 0.5523 = 5523	
Year 5	£10,000 × 0.4761 = 4761	
Present value of future cash-flows		£27,809.2
Net present value of scheme		−£2,190.8

In this calculation the discount figure of 0.8621 in year 1, and those for the other years, are obtained from discount tables like those in the Appendix. The relevant table is the 16 per cent table, and the column used is 'Present value of £1'. This process can be considerably speeded up when the same sum of money is involved in each year, because it is then possible to use the 'Present value of £1 received at the end of period' column just once, as has been done in Solution 26.

The present value of the future cash-flows is less than the outlay of £30,000, which means that the scheme is not making the required 16 per cent on the investment and should not go forward for further consideration. This approach to capital rationing is frequently employed because it reviews the whole scheme and recognises the time-value of money. Tables are prepared showing the appropriate rate by which to multiply at various time-intervals and costs of money.

There is a growing tendency for organisations to use a combination of pay-back and net present value in capital rationing when preparing their capital budgets, but it should be borne in mind that although capital budgeting is essential, a great deal of capital expenditure takes place on the basis of pure necessity rather than because it has been planned for. Machinery breaks down or has to be replaced by new technology, so it should always be remembered that the budget is a plan and not a straitjacket. Different people need different things to help them in their planning, decision-making and control, and it is essential that the management information system gives the right information to the right people and at the right time. The personnel manager needs to keep in mind the criteria that have to be met before schemes requiring capital expenditure are agreed – otherwise all proposals for capital expenditure in the department may be rejected. The effective manager will ensure that the department proposals for capital expenditure meet the required pay-back, rate of return or discounted cash-flow requirements. It is no use to propose outlay on new equipment that will produce training more effectively if the pay-back is five years while the organisation requires three years. Neither would a return of 8 per cent be considered if the organisation expects 10 per cent. To keep submitting schemes that fail to meet the hurdle rates simply ruins the credibility of the department and is in no one's interest because the undertaking as a whole suffers from the inefficiencies of a major constituent.

Work through Exercises 23 and 24 and compare your answers with the sample ones at the back of the book.

COST-BENEFIT ANALYSIS

Cost-benefit analysis is based on the concept of social costs and benefits. For example, a factory owner may pollute the atmosphere with the waste material from the manufacturing process, which would be a social cost. The owner may then build a beautiful house which improves the view for the general population, which is a social benefit. The difficulty lies in valuing the cost and benefit to see which is greater.

Cost-benefit analysis methods are advocated for dealing with capital projects in which investments are large and indivisible, group wants are catered for, and economic prices are not charged to consumers for their use of the final output. Viewed as a purely commercial proposition from the point of view of London Transport, the Jubilee Line is not attractive, although if fares could be charged at an economic rate it could be a profitable investment. In attempting to calculate the costs and benefits of the Jubilee Line, the general headings used would have been:

		£m	Present value at x% discount
Costs:	Annual working costs		
Benefits:	Traffic diverted to Jubilee Line		
	(1) Underground time, comfort		
	(2) Railways' time		
	(3) Buses' time		
	(4) Motorists' time, cost		
	(5) Pedestrians' time		

This would be the skeleton of the final appraisal, and you can see the problems involved in putting a monetary value on many of the benefits as well as in arriving at an appropriate rate of discount. The fact that cost-benefit is difficult to apply does not mean that it should be ignored. It is in fact used frequently where major public works are considered – but entrepreneurs are still rather inclined to ignore it.

Exercise 23
Green is concerned about production costs and after extensive enquiries has identified a new machine that will carry out the required process much more effectively than his present one. The machine costs £80,000 and will last for eight years, during which time running costs and maintenance will be reduced by £10,000 a year and there will be a saving on materials of £4,000 a year. Would you encourage Green to buy the machine if the only consideration was a financial one and the cost of money was 15 per cent?

Exercise 24

A local authority has decided that the heating costs of the personnel department are excessive and has received tenders for insulating the building. The costs of insulation are £130,000, inclusive of double-glazing, and it is expected that the benefits will last for 15 years, after which the department will move to new premises. The estimated savings from the insulation are £16,000 a year and the cost of capital is 8 per cent. Should the insulation be undertaken on the basis of the financial information provided?

What are the four methods of justifying capital expenditure?

What is the most common reason for capital expenditure?

How is the pay-back calculated?

How is the accounting rate of return calculated?

Which method of ranking capital schemes is most commonly employed?

Ascertain the method(s) of ranking capital schemes employed in your organisation. What are they, and how is the appropriate return arrived at?

Appendix

DISCOUNTED CASH FLOW: SELECTED TABLES

Year	Amount to which £1 will accumulate	Present value of £1	Present value of £1 received at end of period	Present value of £1 received continuously	Amount received at end of year which will recover initial investment of £1	Amount received continuously which will recover initial investment of £1	Year
8 per cent rate of return							
1	1.0800	0.9259	0.9259	0.9625	1.0800	1.0390	1
2	1.1664	0.8573	1.7833	1.8537	0.5608	0.5395	2
3	1.2597	0.7938	2.5771	2.6789	0.3880	0.3733	3
4	1.3605	0.7350	3.3121	3.4429	0.3019	0.2905	4
5	1.4693	0.6806	3.9927	4.1504	0.2505	0.2409	5
6	1.5869	0.6302	4.6229	4.8054	0.2163	0.2081	6
7	1.7138	0.5835	5.2064	5.4120	0.1921	0.1848	7
8	1.8509	0.5403	5.7466	5.9736	0.1740	0.1674	8
9	1.9990	0.5002	6.2469	6.4936	0.1601	0.1540	9
10	2.1589	0.4632	6.7101	6.9750	0.1490	0.1434	10
11	2.3316	0.4289	7.1390	7.4209	0.1401	0.1348	11
12	2.6182	0.3971	7.5361	7.8337	0.1327	0.1277	12
13	2.7196	0.3677	7.9038	8.2159	0.1265	0.1217	13
14	2.9372	0.3405	8.2442	8.5698	0.1213	0.1167	14
15	3.1722	0.3152	8.5595	8.8975	0.1168	0.1124	15
16	3.4259	0.2919	8.8514	9.2009	0.1150	0.1087	16
17	3.7000	0.2703	9.1216	9.4818	0.1096	0.1055	17
18	3.9960	0.2502	9.3719	9.7420	0.1067	0.1026	18
19	4.3157	0.2317	9.6036	9.9828	0.1041	0.1002	19
20	4.6610	0.2145	9.8181	10.2058	0.1019	0.0980	20
21	5.0338	0.1987	10.0168	10.4123	0.0998	0.0960	21
22	5.4365	0.1838	10.2007	10.6035	0.0980	0.0943	22
23	5.8715	0.1703	10.3711	10.7806	0.0964	0.0928	23
24	6.3412	0.1577	10.5288	10.9445	0.0950	0.0914	24
25	6.8485	0.1460	10.6748	11.0963	0.0937	0.0901	25
15 per cent rate of return							
1	1.1500	0.8696	0.8696	0.9333	1.1500	1.0715	1
2	1.3225	0.7561	1.6257	1.7448	0.6151	0.5731	2
3	1.5209	0.6575	2.2832	2.4505	0.4380	0.4081	3
4	1.7490	0.5718	2.8550	3.0641	0.3503	0.3264	4

Year	Amount to which £1 will accumulate	Present value of £1	Present value of £1 received at end of period	Present value of £1 received continuously	Amount received at end of year which will recover initial investment of £1	Amount received continuously which will recover initial investment of £1	Year
5	2.0114	0.4972	3.3522	3.5977	0.2983	0.2780	5
6	2.3131	0.4323	3.7845	4.0617	0.2642	0.2462	6
7	2.6600	0.3759	4.1604	4.4652	0.2404	0.2240	7
8	3.0590	0.3269	4.4873	4.8160	0.2229	0.2076	8
9	3.5179	0.2843	4.7716	5.1211	0.2096	0.1953	9
10	4.0456	0.2472	5.0188	5.3864	0.1993	0.1857	10
11	4.6524	0.2149	5.2337	5.6171	0.1911	0.1780	11
12	5.3503	0.1869	5.4206	5.8177	0.1845	0.1719	12
13	6.1528	0.1625	5.5831	5.9921	0.1791	0.1669	13
14	7.0757	0.1413	5.7245	6.1438	0.1747	0.1628	14
15	8.1371	0.1229	5.8474	6.2757	0.1710	0.1593	15
16	9.3576	0.1069	5.9542	6.3904	0.1679	0.1565	16
17	10.7613	0.0929	6.0472	6.4901	0.1654	0.1541	17
18	12.3755	0.0808	6.1280	6.5769	0.1632	0.1520	18
19	14.2318	0.0703	6.1982	6.6523	0.1613	0.1503	19
20	16.3665	0.0611	6.2593	6.7178	0.1598	0.1489	20
21	18.8215	0.0531	6.3125	6.7749	0.1584	0.1476	21
22	21.6447	0.0462	6.3587	6.8245	0.1573	0.1465	22
23	24.8915	0.0402	6.3988	6.8676	0.1563	0.1456	23
24	28.6252	0.0349	6.4338	6.9051	0.1554	0.1448	24
25	32.9190	0.0304	6.4641	6.9377	0.1547	0.1441	25

16 per cent rate of return

Year	Amount to which £1 will accumulate	Present value of £1	Present value of £1 received at end of period	Present value of £1 received continuously	Amount received at end of year which will recover initial investment of £1	Amount received continuously which will recover initial investment of £1	Year
1	1.1600	0.8621	0.8621	0.9293	1.1600	1.0760	1
2	1.3456	0.7432	1.6052	1.7305	0.6230	0.5779	2
3	1.5609	0.6407	2.2459	2.4211	0.4453	0.4130	3
4	1.8106	0.5523	2.7982	3.0165	0.3574	0.3315	4
5	2.1003	0.4761	3.2743	3.5298	0.3054	0.2833	5
6	2.4364	0.4104	3.6847	3.9722	0.2714	0.2517	6
7	2.8262	0.3538	4.0386	4.3537	0.2476	0.2297	7
8	3.2784	0.3050	4.3436	4.6825	0.2302	0.2136	8
9	3.8030	0.2630	4.6065	4.9660	0.2171	0.2014	9
10	4.4114	0.2267	4.8332	5.2103	0.2069	0.1919	10

Solutions to problems and exercises

SOLUTIONS TO CHAPTER 4 EXERCISES

Solution 1

Balance sheet of Sacha as at 5 June

Assets		Liabilities	
Current assets:			
Bank	£60,000	Capital	£60,000

Solution 2

Balance sheet of Sacha as at 6 June

Assets		Liabilities	
Fixed assets:		Capital	£60,000
Premises	£80,000	Loan	40,000
Current assets:			
Bank	20,000		
	£100,000		£100,000

It is assumed that the business borrowed the £40,000, and not Sacha. Had Sacha borrowed the money, then the capital would have become £100,000, and no loan would have appeared.

Solution 3

Balance sheet of Sacha as at 7 June

Assets			Liabilities	
Fixed assets:			Capital	£61,500
Premises	£80,000		Loan	40,000
Fixtures/fittings	8,000			
Motor vehicle	1,500			
		£89,500		
Current assets:				
Bank		12,000		
		£101,500		£101,500

You can see that the capital has increased by £1,500. This is because the van that the owner has brought into the business becomes part of the capital, even though it has not been paid for. The bank balance is reduced by the £8,000 paid for the fixtures and fittings.

Solution 4

Balance sheet of Sacha as at 8 June

Assets			Liabilities	
Fixed assets:			Capital	£61,500
Premises	£80,000		Loan	40,000
Fixtures/fittings	8,000			
Motor vehicle	1,500			
		£89,500		
Current assets:			Current liabilities:	
Inventory	30,000		Creditors	20,000
Bank	2,000			
		32,000		
		£121,500		£121,500

The creditors of £20,000 appear as a current liability, and the bank balance is reduced by the £10,000 paid, to £2,000. The inventory of £30,000 is a current asset.

Solution 5

Balance sheet of Sacha as at 9 June

Assets			Liabilities	
Fixed assets:			Capital	£61,500
Premises	£80,000		Reserves:	
Fixtures/fittings	8,000		Retained profit	40,000
Motor vehicle	1,500		Loan	40,000
		£89,500		
Current assets:			Current liabilities:	
Inventory	10,000		Creditors	20,000
Debtors	50,000			
Bank	12,000			
		72,000		
		£161,500		£161,500

The retained profit of £40,000 under 'Reserves' on the Liabilities side is the profit made on the sale. On the Assets side, the changes take place in the Current assets section, where inventory is reduced by £20,000 to £10,000, the bank balance is increased by £10,000 to £12,000, and debtors for the credit sales of £50,000 appear.

Solution 6

Balance sheet of Sacha as at 10 June

Assets			Liabilities	
Fixed assets:			Authorised and	
Premises	£80,000		issued share capital:	
Fixtures/fittings	8,000		203,000 shares at 50p	£101,500
Motor vehicle	1,500			
		89,500	Loan	40,000
Current assets:			Current liabilities:	
Inventory	10,000		Creditors	20,000
Debtors	50,000			
Bank	12,000			
		72,000		
		£161,500		£161,500

The capital and reserves have been replaced by the authorised and issued share capital. The vertical form of the balance sheet would be:

Balance sheet of Sacha as at 10 June

	£	£
Fixed assets:		
Premises	80,000	
Fixtures and fittings	8,000	
Motor vehicle	1,500	
		£89,500
Current assets:		
Inventory	10,000	
Debtors	50,000	
Bank	12,000	
	72,000	
Less Current liabilities:		
Creditors	20,000	
Working capital		52,000
Net capital employed		£141,500
Less Loan		40,000
		101,500
Financed by:		
Authorised and issued share capital:		
203,000 shares at 50p each		£101,500

SOLUTIONS TO CHAPTER 5 EXERCISES

Solution 7

Trading and profit and loss account of Thomas
for the first four weeks

	£	£
Sales		4,240
Cost of goods sold:		
Opening inventory	0	
Add Inventory purchased	2,600	
	2,600	
Less Closing inventory	120	
Cost of goods sold		2,480
Gross profit		1,760
Less Expenses:		
Rent of yard	160	
Weekend help	180	
Obstruction fines	140	
Depreciation:		
Stall	$\left.\begin{array}{c}20\\7\end{array}\right\}$ 27	
Scales		507
Net profit		1,253

Cash statement

	£	£
Opening balance		£5,000
Add Money received from sales		4,240
		9,240
Less Payments:		
Rent of yard	120	
Help	180	
Fines	140	
Scales	586	
Stall	1,140	
Fruit	2,600	
		4,766
Closing cash in hand		4,474

Balance sheet of Thomas as at the end of the first four weeks

	£	£		£
Fixed assets:			Capital	5,000
Scales	586		Reserves:	
Less depreciation	7		Retained profit	1,253
		£579		
Stall	1,140			
Less depreciation	20			
		1,120		
		1,699		
Current assets:			Current liabilities:	
Inventory	120		Rent due	40
Cash	4,474			
		4,594		
		6,293		6,293

Although a profit of £1,253 has been earned, the cash balance has fallen from £5,000 to £4,474. This means that the business has not generated enough funds for its needs, mainly owing to the purchase of the fixed assets. The depreciation was calculated as follows:

Stall cost	£1,140
Less scrap value	100
	£1,040

divided by life, which is four years, giving 4 × 13 (which is the number of four-week periods in a year) = 52 periods. We then have:

$$\frac{1,040}{52} = £20 \text{ per four-week period}$$

Scales cost	£586
Less scrap value	40
	£546

divided by life, which is six years, giving:

$$\frac{546}{(6 \times 13)} = \frac{546}{78} = £7 \text{ per four-week period}$$

The closing stock is valued at the lower of cost or current market value. The rent of £160 is the rent that should be paid – ie four weeks at £40 per week, whether or not this is actually paid.

Solution 8

Trading and profit and loss account of Thomas
for the second four weeks

	£	£	£
Sales			5,000
Cost of goods sold:			
Opening inventory		120	
Add Inventory purchased		3,900	
		4,020	
Less Closing inventory		400	
			3,620
Gross profit			1,380
Less Expenses:			
Rent		160	
Fines		260	
Help		180	
Depreciation:			
Stall	20		
Scales	7		
		27	
Insurance premium*		16	
			643
Net profit			737

* The insurance premium is derived as one thirteenth of the £208 paid.

Cash statement

	£	£
Opening balance		£4,474
Add money received from sales		5,000
		9,474
Less Payments:		
Rent	120	
Fines	260	
Help	180	
Household expenses	400	
Fruit	3,900	
Insurance	208	
		5,068
Closing cash in hand		4,406

*Balance sheet of Thomas
as at the end of the second four weeks*

	£	£		£	£
Fixed assets:			Capital		5,000
Scales	586		Reserves:		
Less depreciation	14		Retained profit		
		572	First four weeks	1,253	
Stall	1,140		Second four weeks	737	
Less depreciation	40			1,990	
		1,100			
		1,672	Less Household		
			money (drawings)	400	
					1,590
Current assets:			Current liabilities:		
Insurance pre-paid	192		Rent due		80
Inventory	400				
Cash	4,406				
		4,998			
		6,670			6,670

A further profit of £737 has been made in the second four weeks but the cash balance has been reduced by £68, owing largely to the drawings and increased inventory. Generally, it is bad to remove all the profit from a business, but £400 drawings seem reasonable out of a profit of £737, particularly as there is a large sum of money in the business.

Solution 9

*Trading and profit and loss account of Thomas
for the third four weeks*

	£	£	£
Sales			£6,000
Less Cost of goods sold:			
Opening inventory		400	
Add Purchases of fruit		5,000	
		5,400	
Deduct Closing inventory		600	
			4800
Gross profit			1,200
Less Expenses:			
Rent		160	
Fines		300	
Help		180	
Depreciation:			
Stall	20		
Scales	7		
		27	
Insurance		16	
			683
Net operating profit			517
Loss on sale of stall			280
Net profit			237

The operating profit is the profit from normal business operations and excludes unusual or extraordinary items like the profit or loss on the sale of fixed assets. The accounting convention of anticipating losses has been followed by making a provision for the expected fine.

Sale of stall	£
Original cost of stall	1,140
Less total depreciation (20 × 3)	60
Book value of the stall	1,080
Proceeds of the sale	800
Loss on the sale	£280

Cash statement

	£	£
Opening balance		4,406
Add sales receipts		6,000
Receipt from sale of stall		800
		11,206
Deduct payments:		
Delivery van	5,100	
Fruit	5,000	
Household expenses	600	
Rent	200	
Help	180	
		11,080
Closing cash in hand		126

A further operating profit of £517 has seen the cash balance reduced to £126 because of the purchase of the delivery van. Thomas will have to go through a period of consolidation if he is to stabilise his cash situation.

Balance sheet of Thomas
as at the end of the third four weeks

	£	£		£	£	£
Fixed assets:			Capital Reserves:			£5,000
Van		5,100	Retained profit			
Scales	586		First four weeks		1,253	
Less depreciation	21		Second four weeks		737	
		565	Third four weeks		237	
					2,227	
			Less drawings			
			Second four weeks	400		
			Third four weeks	600		
					1,000	
						1,227
Current assets:			Current liabilities:			
Insurance pre-paid	176		Rent due		40	
Inventory	600		Fine pending		300	
Cash	126					340
		902				
		6,567				£6,567

Solution 10

Trading and profit and loss account of Thomas
for the fourth four weeks

	£	£	£
Sales			6,500
Cost of goods sold:			
Opening inventory		600	
Add Purchases of fruit and vegetables		6,500	
		7,100	
Deduct Closing inventory		1,700	
			5,400
Gross profit			1,100
Add Overprovision for fine recovered			160
Deduct Expenses:			
Rent		160	
Help		180	
Vehicle running		100	
Vehicle licence*		10	
Insurance		16	
Depreciation:			
Vehicle	110		
Scales	7		
		117	583
Net profit			677

*The vehicle licence of £10 is derived as one-thirteenth of £130.

Cash statement

	£	£
Opening balance		126
Add Sales receipts		6,100
		6,226
Deduct Payments:		
Inventory purchased for cash	3,500	
Payments to creditor for inventory	1,800	
Vehicle running expenses paid	100	
Vehicle licence purchased	130	
Rent	160	
Help	180	
Household expenses	659	
Fine	140	
		6,660
Cash overdrawn		(434)

Balance sheet of Thomas as at the end of the fourth four weeks

	£	£		£	£	£
Fixed assets:			Capital Reserves:			5,000
			First four weeks	1,253		
Vehicle	5,100		Second four weeks	737		
Less depreciation	110		Third four weeks	237		
		4,990	Fourth four weeks	677		
Scales	586				2,904	
Less depreciation	28	558	*Less* drawings			
			Second four weeks	400		
			Third four weeks	600		
			Fourth four weeks	650		
					1,650	
						1,254
Current assets:			Current liabilities:			
Insurance pre-paid	160		Rent due	40		
Inventory	1,700		Creditor	1,200		
Licence	120		Bank overdraft	434		
Debtors	400					
		2,380				1,674
		7,928				7,928

Thomas's profit is £677. The balance sheet shows his financial position at the end of the fourth four weeks, but only on the assumption that the business is going to continue. If he were to close the business and sell his assets, a very different picture could emerge. For example, the vehicle might realise £3,000 instead of the £4,990 shown in the books, and the scales £40 instead of the book value of £558. There is a problem with liquidity (ie cash resources enabling a business to pay its way) and Thomas may temporarily have to reduce spending on the family.

SOLUTION TO CHAPTER 7 EXERCISES
Solution 11
Thomas's ratios

	Period 1	Period 2	Period 3	Period 4
Net profit as a percentage of the net capital employed $\dfrac{\text{Net profit} \times 100}{\text{Net capital employed}}$	$\dfrac{£1{,}253 \times 100}{£6{,}253} = 20\%$	$\dfrac{£737 \times 100}{£6{,}590} = 11.2\%$	$\dfrac{£237 \times 100}{£6{,}227} = 3.8\%$	$\dfrac{£677 \times 100}{£6{,}254} = 10.8\%$
Gross profit as a percentage of the net capital employed $\dfrac{\text{Gross profit} \times 100}{\text{Net capital employed}}$	$\dfrac{£1{,}760 \times 100}{£6{,}253} = 28\%$	$\dfrac{£1{,}380 \times 100}{£6{,}590} = 20.9\%$	$\dfrac{£1{,}200 \times 100}{£6{,}227} = 10.3\%$	$\dfrac{£1{,}100 \times 100}{£6{,}254} = 17.6\%$
Mark-up $\dfrac{(\text{Selling price} - \text{Cost price}) \times 100}{\text{Cost price}}$	$\dfrac{£1{,}760 \times 100}{£2{,}480} = 71\%$	$\dfrac{£1{,}380 \times 100}{£3{,}620} = 38.1\%$	$\dfrac{£1{,}200 \times 100}{£4{,}800} = 25\%$	$\dfrac{£1{,}100 \times 100}{£5{,}400} = 20.4\%$
Current ratio Current assets : Current liabilities	£4,594 : £40 = 115 : 1	£4,998 : £80 = 62 : 1	£902 : £340 = 2.6 : 1	£2,380 : £1,674 = 1.4 : 1
Quick ratio (acid test) Quick assets: Current liabilities	£4,474 : 40 = 1,119.1 : 1 £4,598 : £80 = 57.4 : 1	£302 : £340 = 0.89 : 1	£680 : £1,674 = 0.4 : 1	
Rate of inventory turnover $\dfrac{\text{Cost of inventory sold}}{\text{Average inventory}}$	$\dfrac{£2{,}480}{£120} = 20.7 \text{ times}$	$\dfrac{£3{,}620}{£260} = 13.9 \text{ times}$	$\dfrac{£4{,}800}{£500} = 9.6 \text{ times}$	$\dfrac{£5{,}400}{£1{,}150} = 4.7 \text{ times}$
Age of debtors Not meaningful in this example.				
Age of creditors Not meaningful in this example.				

SOLUTION TO CHAPTER 10 PROBLEM

Administration

The ratio here will be 100 : 300 (or 1 : 3).

SOLUTIONS TO CHAPTER 11 EXERCISES

Solution 12

Standard cost for one week of five days:

		£
Labour	8 × £40 × 5 =	1,600
Materials	5 × £15 × 5 =	375
Overheads	£60 × 5 =	300
		2,275

Actual cost for one week of five days:

		£
Labour	38 × £41 =	1,558
Materials	28 × £14.50 =	406
Overheads	=	340
		2,304

Total variance: £2,304 − £2,275 = £29 adverse

This represents only 1 per cent of budget and would in practice probably not be investigated further because of time constraints – but we will calculate the individual variances that go to make up the £29.

Labour variances	£
Standard cost	1,600
Actual cost	1,558
	42 favourable

This breaks down into labour rate variance and labour efficiency variance:

Labour rate variance 38 hours × (£40 − £41)	£38 adverse
Labour efficiency variance £40 × (40 − 38) hours	£80 favourable
which nets back to the total labour variance:	£42 favourable

Material variances

Standard cost	£375
Actual cost	406
	£ 32 adverse

This breaks down into material price variance and material usage variances:

Material price variance	
28 × (£15 − £14.50)	£14 favourable
Material usage variance	
£15 × (25 − 28)	£45 adverse
which nets back to the total	
materials variance:	£31 adverse

Overhead variance

This can be dealt with only in total:

Standard cost	£300
Actual cost	340
	£ 40 adverse

Each of these variances should then be discussed in turn and suggestions made on the most appropriate course of action.

Solution 13

Standard cost of a week for 20 delegates

	£
Delegates 20 × £7.20 × 40 =	5,760.00
Trainers 2 × £8.65 × 40 =	692.00
Overheads	1,000.00
	7,452.00
Actual cost of a week for 20 delegates	7,810.80
Adverse variance	358.80

This variance represents 4.8% of standard or accepted cost and may therefore be considered to be within accepted tolerances. However, let us undertake a further investigation. The variances will involve only labour and overheads because there are no materials that have been separately costed.

	£
Actual cost of delegates	5,880
Standard cost of delegates	5,760
Adverse variance	120

Labour rate variance

Actual hours × change in rate
(20 × 42) × 20p =   £168 favourable

Labour efficiency variance

Standard wage per hour × change in hours   £
£7.20 × [(42 − 40) × 20] =   288 adverse

	120 adverse
Actual cost of trainers	730.80
Standard cost of trainers	692.00
Adverse variance	38.80

Labour rate variance

(2 × 42) × 5p =   £4.20 adverse

Labour efficiency variance   £

£8.65 × [(42 − 40) × 2] =   34.60 adverse
                                           38.80 adverse

Overhead variance

$$\frac{\text{Standard overheads} - \text{Actual overhead}}{1,000 \qquad\qquad 1,200} = \qquad \text{£200 adverse}$$

Total variance   £

Labour: trainers	38.80 adverse
Labour: delegates	120.00 adverse
Overheads	200.00 adverse
	358.80 adverse

Solution 14

Points that should be considered include:

• preparation of the planned or standard level of activity

• comparison of the actual activity with the planned activity

- the significance of any variances (differences) obtained
- ascertaining the cause of the variance
- deciding on any necessary corrective action
- taking the necessary action quickly and effectively.

SOLUTIONS TO CHAPTER 12 EXERCISES

Solution 15

If demand fell to 300 hours, the loss would be:

$$(333 \text{ hours} - 300 \text{ hours}) \times 30 = £990$$

This is less than the loss involved in doing nothing, which would be £9,990. In the short run it is therefore better to keep going and look to save costs, increase prices or find new outlets.

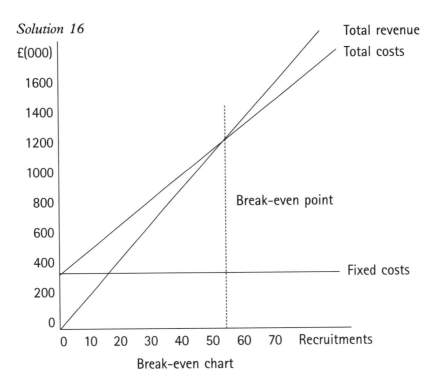

Solution 16

Break-even chart

The break-even point is at 58 units sold.

Total revenue 70 × £25,000 =	£1,750,000
Total cost is £319,000 + (19500 × 70) =	£1,684,000
Profit	£66,000

Solution 17

1 Recruitment

2 Training

3 Establishing departmental contribution.

Solution 18

True cost of buying in	£4,000
Add 25% of £10,000	£2,500
	£6,500

The personnel department therefore is cheaper, because the £10,000 head office costs have to be found whether you buy in or not.

SOLUTIONS TO CHAPTER 13 EXERCISE

Solution 19

Sales budget
Units sold

Week	Planned sales	Actual	Cumulative	Actual
1	50		50	
2	50		100	
3	50		150	
4	50		200	
5	50		250	
6	50		300	
7	50		350	
8	50		400	
9	50		450	
10	50		500	
11	50		550	
12	50		600	

Labour budget

Week	Planned hours	Actual hours	Planned cumulative hours	Actual hours
1	30		30	
2	30		60	
3	30		90	
4	30		120	
5	30		150	
6	30		180	
7	30		210	
8	30		240	
9	30		270	
10	30		300	
11	30		330	
12	30		360	

Materials budget

	Opening balance		Purchases				Use			Closing balance	
Week	Plan	Actual	Plan	Cum.	Actual	Cum.	Plan	Cum.	Actual	Plan	Actual
1	10		25	25			25	25		10	
2	10		25	50			25	50		10	
3	10		25	75			25	75		10	
4	10		25	100			25	100		10	
5	10		25	125			25	125		10	
6	10		25	150			25	150		10	
7	10		25	175			25	175		10	
8	10		25	200			25	200		10	
9	10		25	225			25	225		10	
10	10		25	250			25	250		10	
11	10		25	275			25	275		10	
12	10		25	300			25	300		10	

Expenses budget

			Cumulative	
Week	Planned expenses	Actual	Planned	Actual
1	£40		£ 40	
2	40		80	
3	40		120	
4	40		160	
5	40		200	
6	40		240	
7	40		280	
8	40		320	
9	40		360	
10	40		400	
11	40		440	
12	40		480	

Cash budget

Week:	1	2	3	4	5	6	7	8	9	10	11	12
Opening balance	£400	(£105)	(£610)	(£1,115)	(£1,620)	(£1,125)	(£630)	(£135)	£360	£855	£1,350	£1,845
Add sales receipt					1,000	1,000	1,000	1,000	1,000	1,000	1,000	1,000
Balance	400	(105)	(610)	(1,115)	(620)	(125)	370	865	1,360	1,855	2,350	2,845
Deduct Payments:												
Labour	450	450	450	450	450	450	450	450	450	450	450	450
Materials	15	15	15	15	15	15	15	15	15	15	15	15
Expenses	40	40	40	40	40	40	40	40	40	40	40	40
Total	£505	£505	£505	£505	£505	£505	£505	£505	£505	£505	£505	£505
Balance c/f	(105)	(610)	(1,115)	(1,620)	(1,125)	(630)	(135)	360	855	1,350	1,845	2,340

The cash budget clearly shows a cash-flow deficit for the first seven weeks, rising to a maximum of £1,620 in Week 4. This might necessitate a change in the plan or it might be possible to obtain an overdraft facility of £2,000 for 10 weeks from the bank. This will allow some flexibility if the plan has any errors in it.

Forecast profit and loss account

	£	£
Sales		£12,000
Less Cost of sales:		
Opening inventory	6	
Add Material purchased	180	
	186	
Less Closing inventory	6	
		180
		11,820
Gross profit		
Less Expenses:		
Wages	5,400	
Expenses	480	
		5,880
Net profit		£5,940

Balance sheet as at the end of three months

	£		£
Inventory	6	Capital	406
Debtors	4,000	Profit	5,940
Bank	2,340		
	6,346		6,346

SOLUTIONS TO CHAPTER 14 EXERCISES

Solution 20

If the forecasts are correct and Brown can obtain an overdraft facility of £4,000 for six months, the business seems likely to be successful. It should be borne in mind, however, that in order to produce 10 models he will have to work 80 hours a week and may find that impossible to achieve over a long period of time.

Solution 20

	January	February	March	April	May	June
Opening balance in hand	£2,000				£506	£3,182
(overdrawn)		(£964)	(£3,082)	(£2,170)		
Add Receipts from sales		846	5,076	5,640	5,640	5,640
Total	£2,000	(£118)	£1,994	£3,470	£6,146	£8,822
Less Payments:						
Brown	800	800	800	800	800	800
Wood	1200	1200	1200	1200	1200	1200
Rent	40	40	40	40	40	40
Postage	924	924	924	924	924	924
Rates, etc			1,200			1,200
Equipment						5,000
Total	£2,964	£2,964	£4,164	£2,964	£2,964	£9,164
Balance c/f in hand				£506	£3,182	
(overdrawn)	(£964)	(£3,082)	(£2,170)			(£342)

Solution 21

	July	August	September	October	November	December
	£	£	£	£	£	£
Opening Balance	3,000	2,380	4,760	(10,660)	(4,600)	4,260
Sales receipts	9,600	11,200	12,800	14,400	15,200	10,400
	12,600	13,580	17,560	3,740	10,600	14,660
Payments:						
Labour	4,000	2,600	2,200	2,000	1,800	1,400
Materials	3,600	4,080	4,320	4,800	3,120	2,640
Variable expenses	720	800	520	440	400	360
	1,600	1,040	880	800	720	560
Fixed expenses	300	300	300	300	300	300
Capital expenditure	–	–	20,000	–	–	–
	10,220	8,820	28,220	8,340	6,340	5,260
Balance carried forward	2,380	4,760	(10,660)	(4,600)	4,260	9,400

Solution 22

	November	December	January	February	March	April
	£	£	£	£	£	£
Opening Balance	(1,050)	(2,100)	(500)	(1,575)	6,575	350
Cash Receipts	5,400	9,000	6,300	20,700	3,600	7,200
Received from Debtors	800	600	1,000	700	2,300	400
Total cash available	5.150	7,150	6,800	19,825	12,475	7,950
Cash purchases	2,250	3,750	2,625	8,625	1,500	3,000
Previous Credit Purchases	3,000	2,250	3,750	2,625	8,625	1,500
Wages	2,000	2,000	2,000	2,000	2,000	2,000
	7,250	8,000	8,375	13,250	12,125	6,500
Balance carried forward	(2,100)	(500)	(1,575)	6,575	350	1,450

Note 1 The opening balance of (£1,050) overdrawn comes from the overdraft shown on the opening balance sheet.

Note 2 Cash receipts are obtained by taking 90 per cent of November sales of £6,000, which gives £5,400. The other 10 per cent is shown as receipts from debtors, £600, in December.

Note 3 Receipts from debtors, £800, comes from the debtors shown in the opening balance sheet.

Note 4 Cash payments, £2,250, is derived from the fact that the gross profit margin is 25 per cent of the selling price, which is 25 per cent of £6,000 (= £1,500). This means that the cost of sales, ie purchases, is £4,500. As 50 per cent of the purchases is paid for straight away and 50 per cent in the next month, £2,250 is therefore cash purchases this month (November), and £2,250 previous cash purchases next month (December).

Note 5 The previous credit purchases for November, £3,000, come from the creditors in the opening balance sheet.

NB: The processes detailed above are followed each month through to June.

SOLUTIONS TO CHAPTER 16 EXERCISES

Solution 23

Pay-back

Cost of new machine		£80,000
Annual savings	£14,000 p.a.	
Pay-back	<u>5.7 years</u>	

If Green is looking for a three-year pay-back, the scheme would be rejected. The decision would be reversed, however, if he required a six-year pay-back.

Accounting rate of return

Cost of new machine		£80,000
Average annual savings	£14,000	

Because the same sum of money is saved each year, the average annual saving is the same as the annual saving.

Rate of return: $\dfrac{£14,000 \times 100}{£80,000} = 17.5\%$

If Green requires a 15 per cent rate of return, this scheme could go forward.

Discounted cash-flow					£
Cost of new machine					80,000
Savings: £				£	
1	14,000	×	0.8696	=	12,174.4
2	14,000	×	0.7561	=	10,585.4
3	14,000	×	0.6575	=	9,205.0
4	14,000	×	0.5718	=	8,005.2
5	14,000	×	0.4972	=	6,960.8
6	14,000	×	0.4323	=	6,052.2
7	14,000	×	0.3759	=	5,262.6
8	14,000	×	0.3269	=	4,576.6

Present value of future cash flows	<u>62,822.2</u>
Net present value of scheme	<u>−17,177.8</u>

The scheme would be rejected on this criterion, because it would not make the 15 per cent required, but there may be criteria other than the financial one that could make Green decide to go ahead anyway – for example, his competitive position.

In using the discounted cash-flow (DCF) approach it is possible to take a short-cut when the same sum of money is involved each year. So far we have used the 'Present value of £1' column, but we could use the 'Present value of £1 received at end of period' column, when we have:

Cost of new machine		£80,000
Savings	£14,000 × 4,4873	
Present value of future cash flows		62,822.2
Net present value of the scheme		−17,177.8

It should be emphasised that this approach can be employed *only* when the *same* sum of money is involved each year.

Solution 24

Pay-back

Cost of insulation		£130,000
Savings	£16,000 p.a	
Pay-back:	$\dfrac{£130,000}{£16,000}$	= 8.1 years

If the authority requires a back-back of five years, this scheme would be rejected, but if the criterion was 10 years, it could go forward.

Accounting rate of return

Cost of insulation		£130,000
Average annual savings		£16,000
Rate of return:	$\dfrac{£16,000 \times 100}{£130,000}$	= 12.3%

If a return of 8 per cent is required, this scheme could proceed, but one of 14 per cent would cause it to be rejected.

Discounted cash-flow

Cost of insulation	£130,000
Savings: £16,000 × 8.5595	
Present value of future cash flows	136,952
Net present value of the scheme	+£6,952

The scheme would be accepted because it would make more than the 8 per cent required.

Glossary

Accounting period Normally 12 months, as far as the financial accounts are concerned, to coincide with the tax year. So far as the management accounts are concerned it can be any period ranging from one week to one year. It is generally thought necessary to provide management with information at least once every four weeks.

Acid test Test of the ability of an organisation to pay its way in the short term, given by the ratio of quick assets to current liabilities.

Added value The value an organisation adds to bought-in goods and services. It goes to meet wages and then profits.

Articles of association Internal rules that state the rights and duties of directors and shareholders of a company.

Assets Items belonging to the organisation that have either a long-term or a short-term value. Those having a long-term value are items like machinery and plant. They are called fixed assets.

Authorised capital The total amount of shares that the organisation is authorised to issue in order to raise money. The authorised capital is subject to stamp duty, and so organisations do not state high authorised capital figures when they are first formed. The authorised share capital is not set for all time, and can be varied if necessary.

Book value The value at which an asset is shown in the balance sheet.

Budget A budget is a forecast or estimate of events over a stated future interval of time, eg one year, five years, six months, or any other time.

Capital employed The total of the assets owned. The net capital employed is more usually used in calculating ratios and is the total assets less the current liabilities.

Capital items Items that last for several years. Examples are machinery used in manufacture, motor vehicles, land and buildings.

Credit terms Providing or receiving goods or services for which payment will be made at a later date.

Current assets Assets that are normally used up in one financial period and change from day to day.

Current liabilities Liabilities that must be settled within a short time; they fluctuate from day to day.

Current ratio Measure of the organisation's ability to pay its way in the period between about three and nine months in the future. Given by the ratio of current assets to current liabilities.

Debenture A certificate issued by a company acknowledging a debt.

Depreciation Method of allocating the cost of a fixed asset over its useful life.

Discounted cash-flow (DCF) Future cash flows discounted to give their present value.

Dividend Distribution of profits to the shareholders. Usually expressed as a dividend of xp in the £ on the nominal value of shares.

Earnings Money received or due for goods or services provided by the organisation.

Equity The equity of the business is the part that belongs to the owners. It is what remains after all outside interests have received their money.

Expenses Money paid or due to be paid by the organisation for revenue, goods or services it has received.

Fixed assets Assets held for many years to earn profits. Examples are land and buildings, or plant and machinery.

Fixed overheads   Expenses that do not vary with the level of activity.

Gearing   Relationship between the share capital and loan capital of a business.

Goodwill   The excess over the book value of a business that is received when the business is sold.

Historical cost   The cost at which the assets were obtained.

Income statement   Used to calculate the profit or loss of an organisation in an accounting period. Made up of: (1) The *manufacturing account*, showing the costs of goods made; (2) The *trading account*, showing the gross profit or loss; the difference between the cost price and selling price of the goods; (3) the *profit and loss account*, showing the net profit or loss.

Inventory   Stock.

Issued capital   The shares that have been issued by the organisation in order to raise money.

Job cost   The cost of a single job or operation.

Liabilities   Money that the organisation owes.

Limited company   A limited company is a business the owners of which have limited liability in the case of failure.

Liquidity   Cash resource enabling the business to pay its way.

Long-term liabilities   Long-term debts.

Marginal cost   The cost of one more unit.

Margin of safety   The excess of sales over the break-even point.

Memorandum of association   The formal, written constitution of the company.

Net assets   Total assets less current liabilities.

Net capital employed   The resources that are employed

in the business for more than one year, enabling the return on the long-term investment to be found. The net capital employed is calculated by deducting the current liabilities from the total assets.

NPV Net present value of a scheme.

Ordinary shares Share capital that has a fixed rate of dividend, and receives its dividends before the rest of the share capital. Usually carry voting rights

Prime costs Direct materials, direct labour and direct expenses added together.

Private sector Non-government sector.

Profit Surplus of earnings over expenses.

Public limited company (plc) Limited company that conforms to European Union regulations.

Public sector Government sector, either central or local.

Quick assets Those that are quickly and easily realisable – normally debtors and cash.

Quick ratio Acid test.

Reserves Profits that are retained in the business – rarely cash.

Retained profits Reserves.

Revenue items Items that are completely used up or discharged in one year. Examples are salaries, wages, heating, raw materials.

Revenue reserves Reserves distributable to shareholders.

Share capital The amount received from the shareholders of the business for issued shares at the nominal value.

Share premium A capital reserve (one which cannot be distributed to the shareholders) created when the company sells its shares at a price in excess of the nominal value.

Sole trader A business owned by a person with unlimited liability.

Standard cost   Predetermined or expected cost.

Stock turnover   The number of times the stock is turned over in a financial period, given by the ratio of cost of goods sold to cost of stock.

Turnover   Total sales value.

Variable overheads   Indirect expenses that vary with the level of activity.

Variances   Differences between standard and actual performance.

Working capital   Capital needed to keep the business operating until more money is obtained from operations. It corresponds to current assets minus current liabilities.

Bibliography

DAVIES, D. B. *The Art of Managing Finance*. 3rd edn. London, McGraw-Hill, 1997.

DYSON, J. R. *Accounting for Non-Accounting Students*. 3rd edn. Singapore, Pitman, 1994.

HATHERLEY, D. *Accounting for Business Activity*. London, Pitman, 1993.

HENLEY, D. *et al*. *Public Sector Accounting and Financial Control*. 4th edn. London, Chapman & Hall, 1992.

Key British Enterprises (Annual edition). London, Dun and Bradstreet.

MCLANEY, E. AND ATTRILL, P. *Accounting: An introduction*. Hemel Hempstead, Prentice-Hall, 1999.

PIGGEY, A. *Finance and Accounting*. London, Pitman, 1998.

WATTS, B. *Business Finance*. 8th edn. London, Pitman, 1997.

WATTS, J. *Accounting in the Business Environment*. London, Pitman, 1993.

Professional standards index

This index cross-references to chapters in the text the main subject areas as set out in the Professional Standards of the Institute of Personnel and Development for *Managing Financial Information.*

UNIT	INDEX OF COMPETENCES	CHAPTERS
B3	**Manage the use of financial resources**	
Element B.3.1	Make recommendations for expenditure	12, 16, 17
Element B.3.2	Control expenditure against budgets	3, 7, 9, 11, 13, 14, 15
B5	**Secure financial resources for your organisation's plans**	
Element B.5.1	Review the generation and allocation of financial resources	4, 5, 6, 8, 9, 10, 14, 15
Element B.5.2	Evaluate proposals for expenditure	3, 7, 12, 16, 17
Element B.5.3	Obtain financial resources for your organisation's activities	8, 13, 14, 17

Index

ABC *see* activity-based costing
absorption costing 88–95
accounting periods 169
accounting principles 39–42
accounting rate of return 139
accruals 34
acid test 66–7, 69–70, 169
activity-based costing 95–6
activity budgets 116
activity ratios 67–70, 76
added value 45, 169
administration budgets 117
adverse variance
    labour costs 101
    material costs 102
age
    of creditors 69, 76
    of debtors 69, 76
    of inventory 68, 76
annual general meetings 3
annual reports 3
apportionment of overheads
    89–91, 93–6
articles of association 3, 9, 169
assets
    balance sheets 24, 33–4, 35
    definition of term 169
    fixed assets *see* fixed assets
    liquidity ratios 66
    management of 10–11
    net assets 171
    see also uses of finance
attainable standards 99
auditors' reports 3, 4
authorised capital 34–5, 169

balance sheets 22–4, 28–37, 132
    Sainsbury case study 72
bank balance

balance sheets 28, 29, 30, 31,
    33
    and profit 42–3
book value 169
borrowed monies 9, 10, 15–17
    balance sheets 33, 34, 44
    cash-flow problems 67
break-even point 108, 109, 110
budget centres 129–30
budgeting 21–2, 23, 115–20
    capital budgeting 118, 136–42
    cash budgets 26, 27, 46, 118,
    122–8
    definition of term 169
    master budgets 22–7, 119,
    129–35
Business Expansion Scheme 16
Business Names Act 1985 2, 3

capital
    balance sheets 28, 29, 33,
    34–5
    sources and uses of 13–18
capital budgeting 118, 136–42
capital employed 169–70
    see also net capital employed
capital investment decisions 10,
    80–81, 136, 141
capital rationing methods 81,
    136–40, 141–2
    accounting rate of return 139
    cost-benefit analysis 141–2
    discounted cash flow 139–40
    pay-back 136, 138
capital transactions, distinguished
    from revenue transactions 42
cash budgets 26, 27, 46, 118,
    122–8
cash-flow management 5

see also debtors; liquidity
cash statements 26–7, 46–9
closing inventory 25, 44, 55–6
commercial public corporations 3,
4
companies, legal framework of 3
Companies Act 1985 3
Companies House 3
company names 2, 3
company secretaries 3
competitiveness, pricing strategies
58–9
conservatism 41
consistency in accounting method
40–41
contribution, marginal costing 81,
108–11
control ratio *see* ratios
convertible loans 15
cost accounts, relationship with
financial accounts 83–4, 85
cost-benefit analysis 141–2
cost of human resources ratios
79–80
cost prices 58, 64–5
cost reductions 59
costing 81, 83–7
absorption costing 88–95
marginal costing 106–12
standard costing 97–105
credit transactions 42–3, 46, 48,
69–70
creditors
balance sheets 31, 32, 33, 34
speed of payment 69, 76, 123
current assets 10, 170
balance sheets 24, 32, 34
liquidity ratios 66
current liabilities
balance sheets 24, 34, 35
definition of term 170
liquidity ratios 66
current ratios 66, 75, 170
currentness of information 11, 21

death
of company owners 3

of a partner 2
of a sole trader 2
debentures 170
debtors 6, 7
balance sheets 31, 32, 33
speed of collection 69, 76
demand, activity budgeting 116
depreciation
cost apportionment 89, 91
definition of term 170
manufacturing accounts 57
profit and loss accounts
40–41, 42, 44, 47
direct costs 85
direct expenses, manufacturing
accounts 56
direct manufacturing wages 54, 56
directors 3, 13
discounted cash-flow 139–40,
144–5, 170
dividends 170
double-entry book-keeping 32

earnings, definition of term 170
efficiency ratios 67–70, 76
equity capital 6, 13–15, 170
balance sheets 28, 33, 35
expenses
budgets 118–19
definition of term 170
manufacturing accounts 55,
56
profit and loss accounts 42, 44

favourable variance
labour costs 101
material costs 102
finance function 9–18
financial accounts, relationship
with cost accounts 83–4, 85
financial budgets 117
financial information systems 11,
20–27
financial managers, role of 9–11
financing 6–7, 9–10, 13–18
financing charges 44, 47
fixed assets

balance sheets 24, 32, 34, 42
and borrowing 17
cash statements 47
definition of term 170
efficiency ratios 76
profit and loss accounts
40–41, 42
fixed costs 85–6, 88
absorption costing 92–3
and marginal costs 106–11
fixed overheads 171
full-cost approach *see* absorption
costing

gearing 9, 17, 67, 75, 171
'goodwill' 24–5, 171
gross profit
profitability ratios 62–3, 64–5,
75
trading accounts 25, 57

heating and lighting
cash statements 47
cost apportionment 89, 91
manufacturing accounts 57
profit and loss accounts 44
highly geared companies 9, 17, 67
historical cost 171

income statements 38, 171
see also trading and profit and
loss accounts
incorporation 3
indirect costs 85
apportionment of 89–96
indirect factory expenses 55, 56
indirect wages 54
information systems *see* financial
information systems
interest cover 67, 75
interest on loans 16, 17, 44, 67.
inventory
balance sheets 29, 30, 31, 33
cash statements 46
manufacturing accounts 55–6
profit and loss accounts 25,
41, 43–4

rate of turnover 68, 76
valuation of 41
investment decisions *see* capital
investment decisions
issued capital 171
issuing houses 14

job cost 171
'just-in-time' inventory
management 68

labour costs 84, 85–6, 88
absorption costing 89, 90, 91
standard costing 100–01, 103
see also wages
labour efficiency variance 100, 101
labour rate variance 100, 101
leverage *see* gearing
liabilities
balance sheets 24, 33, 34, 35
definition of term 171
liquidity ratios 66
see also sources of finance
limited companies 3, 34, 171
limiting factors, budgeting 119–20
liquidity 24, 43, 46–8, 122
definition of term 171
ratios 65–7, 69–70, 75
loans *see* borrowed monies
local authorities 4
funding 18
master budgets 133–5
long-term capital 15–17
long-term liabilities 34, 171
long-term planning 114–15
long-term solvency ratios 67, 75

maintenance costs 88
management information systems
see financial information
systems
manufacturing accounts 54–60,
131
manufacturing costs, and selling-
prices 58–9
margin of safety 171
marginal costing 81, 106–12, 171

'mark-up' 64–5
market share, pricing strategy 58–9
master budgets 22–7, 119, 129–35
matching principle 39
material price variance 101, 102, 103
material usage variance 101–02, 103
materials
    budgets 118
    costing 85, 101–2, 103
    manufacturing accounts 56
    see also raw materials
memorandum of association 3, 9, 171
merchant banks 16
money flow
    in manufacturing concerns 5, 6
    in non-manufacturing concerns 7, 8
monitoring of performance 21
morale, and standard costing systems 98–9, 103

narrative form, balance sheets 34
net assets 171
net capital employed
    balance sheets 34, 35
    definition of term 171–2
    profitability ratios 62–4
net present value (NPV) 81, 139–40, 144–5
net profit
    profit and loss accounts 25, 44, 45, 58
    profitability ratios 63–4, 65, 75

objective-setting 114
off-peak pricing 111
opening balance 122
opening inventory 25, 43, 55
ordinary share capital 13–14, 172
organisational objectives 114

organisational structures 12
overheads
    apportionment of 89–91, 93–6
    manufacturing accounts 55, 56

Partnership Act 1890 2
partnerships 2
pay see labour costs; wages
pay-back 81, 136, 138
payments
    cash budgets 123, 125
    cash statements 46, 47, 48, 49
    speed of 69, 76, 123
pension funds 16
perfect standards 98
permanent capital 13–15, 32–3
personnel budgets 116–17
personnel departments
    cash budgets 124–5, 130
    cash statements 49
personnel ratios 79
planning 20–22, 113–15
    long-term 114–15
    short-term 115
    systems 113–14
    see also budgeting
planning permission 2
preference shares 14
premises, balance sheets 29
pricing 58–9, 64–5
primary ratios 63–4
prime costs 85, 172
private sector
    compared with public sector 5–8
    definition of term 172
    financing 9–10, 13–18
    measures of success 1
    organisational structures 12
    types of organisation 1–3
profit 42–3, 172
    see also net profit; retained profit
profit and loss accounts see trading and profit and loss accounts

profitability
  distinguished from liquidity
    43, 46–8
  ratios 62–5, 75
public limited companies 3, 172
public sector
  compared with private sector
    5–8
  definition of term 172
  financing 10, 18
  measures of success 1
  organisational structures 12
  types of organisation 3–4
  see also local authorities

quick assets 66, 172
quick ratios 66–7, 69–70, 75, 172

rates 89, 91
ratios
  cost of human resources
    79–80
  departmental 79–80
  efficiency 67–70
  liquidity 65–7
  profitability 62–5
  Sainsbury case study 75–6
  sales per employee 76, 78–9
raw materials, manufacturing
    accounts 55–6, 58
  see also materials
receipts
  cash budgets 122–3
  cash statements 46, 48, 49
Registrar of Companies 3
registration of companies 3
research and development costs
    24, 25
reserves 13, 172
  balance sheets 30, 31, 33, 44
resources required by
    organisations 5
retained profits 10, 13, 172
  balance sheets 30, 31, 33
return
  on capital employed 62–4
  on sales 64–5

revenue items 42, 172
revenue reserves 172
risk carried by shareholders 13–14

Sainsbury, J., plc (case study)
    70–76
sales
  per employee 76, 78–9
  profit and loss accounts 42, 43
  profitability ratios 64–5
security on loans 15, 16
selling-prices 58–9, 64–5
semi-variable costs 88
share capital 13–15, 172
  on balance sheets 35
share issues 9, 14
share premium 172
shareholders 3, 13–14
short-term capital 17–18
short-term planning 115
skill of employees, and labour
    variances 103
social costs and benefits 141–2
social service organisations 4
sole traders 2, 172
solvency ratios 67, 75
sources of finance
  balance sheets 28, 29, 30, 31,
    32, 33
  financing 6–7, 9–10, 13–18
spare capacity 111
staff reductions 59, 79
standard costing 97–105
  corrective action 102–3
  labour costs 100–01
  material costs 101–02
  setting standard costs 98–9
stock see inventory
Stock Exchange 3, 13, 14
straight-line approach to
    depreciation 40–41
suppliers see creditors

Tesco 15
theft 58
timeliness of information 11, 21
total costing see absorption costing

trading and profit and loss
     accounts 24–5, 38–45
     forecasts 131
     relationship of manufacturing
     accounts to 54, 57
     Sainsbury case study 71
training
     external marketing of 81
     fixed and variable costs 85–7
     need for 116–17
turnover
     of creditors 69, 76
     of debtors 69, 76
     definition of term 173
     of inventory 68, 76

ultra vires 4, 10
unit costs 58, 59
uses of finance, balance sheets 28,
29, 30, 31, 32, 33

valuation of inventory 41
value-added tax, registration for 2,
     3
variable costs 85, 86, 87, 88
variances 100–03, 173
venture capital 16
vertical form, balance sheets 34

wages
     cash statements 47
     manufacturing accounts 54,
     56
     profit and loss accounts 44
     see also labour costs
working capital 15, 34, 67–8, 173

zero-based budgeting 129–30

The People and Organisations series and Core Management studies

The only route to a professional career in personnel and development is through the achievement of the CIPD's professional standards. One of the three fields that make up these standards, the new Core Management standards define the essentials for competently managing and developing people. They are compatible with an N/SVQ at Level 4 in management.

CIPD Publications has five books in the *People and Organisations* series as textbooks for the new Core Management standards. The texts of these five books and their titles closely follow the Core Management syllabus. The titles of the books are:

Managing Activities	Michael Armstrong
Managing Financial Information	David Davies
Managing in a Business Context	David Farnham
Managing Information and Statistics	Roland and Frances Bee
Managing People	Jane Weightman

Managing in a Business Context
David Farnham

Managing in a Business Context illustrates the framework in which businesses are working in Britain today. Beginning with the nature of strategy and how strategy can be converted into practice, it then considers the issues of wider concern to HR practitioners and business managers in general.

It examines:

- economics, politics and political systems, and their effect on the workplace
- social and legal structures, and how they impinge on the private and public sectors
- the technological revolution and its effect on working practices
- business ethics and the impact of an international climate.

Professor David Farnham holds the chair in Employment Relations at the University of Portsmouth. He has also written *Employee Relations in Context*, published by the CIPD.

1999
£16.99
0 85292 783 5
Paperback
368 pages
246 × 177mm format

Managing Information and Statistics
Roland and Frances Bee

Managing Information and Statistics is a hands-on guide that explains how the apparently esoteric discipline of statistics can be an invaluable management tool. Tables, diagrams and graphs are explained in detail; surveys, forecasting and the principles of relationships between data each have their own sections.

It examines:

- how to produce reports and presentations to the highest standard
- how to use general statistical packages
- how to apply statistical thinking to people-management issues
- how to manage data effectively.

Frances and Roland Bee are experienced training consultants and have written four other highly successful CIPD books – *Training Needs Analysis and Evaluation, Constructive Feedback, Customer Care* and *Project Management*. They are also the authors of *The Complete Learning Evaluation Toolkit,* a looseleaf training resource.

1999
£15.99
0 85292 785 1
Paperback
336 pages
246 × 177mm format

Managing People
Jane Weightman

Managing People is an approachable introduction to working with people and to understanding how people work. It discusses the psychology of the workplace, including its fundamental characteristics, differences between individuals, and how people learn. *Managing People* also studies issues of central concern to all managers, such as performance management, and training and development.

It examines:

- how to motivate your employees
- differing work patterns and their implications for the workplace
- how to manage work-related stress.

Jane Weightman is a psychologist and has been associated with UMIST since 1980. She has carried out research into a wide range of management-related topics and has written widely in a range of journals. Her books include *Competencies in Action* and *Managing People in the Health Service*, both published by the CIPD.

1999
£16.99
0 85292 784 3
Paperback
240 pages
246 × 177mm format